People

CORETTA SCOTT KING Tribute to a Hero

FEBRUARY 13, 2006
Murder in Massachusetts

Who Killed Rachel and Her Baby?

SAG AWARDS Britney Boogies!

ABC's BOB WOODRUFF How He's Recovering

The shocking killing of Rachel Entwistle and her daughter Lillian—and her British husband's strange behavior—trigger an international mystery

---

People

GIBSON'S JULY 28 MUG SHOT

Behind Mel's Meltdown

Arrested for drunken driving, the 'ashamed' actor enters rehab and apologizes for spewing religious slurs

AUGUST 14, 2006

PAM & KID'S WILD, WILD 'WEDDING'!

LINDSAY LOHAN Told To Stop Partying

DEAD OR ALIVE? A Serial Killer's Chilling Photo Album

JUNE 19, 2006

People

CAR CRASH MIX-UP What Went Wrong

Exclusive!

First Baby Pictures!

Brad and Angelina welcome daughter Shiloh

The family in Namibia June 3, 2006

SPECIAL DOUBLE ISSUE

People

BRITNEY'S BABY IT'S A BOY!

STEVE IRWIN Private Family Funeral

ANNA NICOLE Her Son's Tragic Death

BEST (& Worst!) DRESSED

WHAT'S HOT, WHAT'S NOT
Shocking Styles • 308 Celeb Looks

JONBENET'S MOTHER DIES

JULY 10, 2006

People

NICOLE KIDMAN & KEITH URBAN'S

DREAM WEDDING!

He cried, she cried—all about the couple's romantic candlelit ceremony
PLUS Their island honeymoon

Marcia Cross Gets Married

Star Jones WHY I GOT FIRED

APRIL 10, 2006

People

The Minister's Shooting

WHY DID SHE KILL HIM?

THEY SEEMED THE PERFECT COUPLE. THEN, COPS SAY, SHE SHOT HER HUSBAND IN THE BACK
THE STORY OF MATTHEW & MARY WINKLER

Mary and Matthew Winkler with daughters (from left) Brianna, Mary Alice and Patricia

KATIE HOLMES COUNTDOWN TO BABY!

HEATHER & RICHIE OUT AS A FAMILY

$3.69US $4.79CAN
15>
0 72440 10227 9
www.people.com (AOL Keyword: People)

MAY 1, 2006

People

EXCLUSIVE PHOTOS!

Gwyneth Paltrow Meet Baby Moses

It's a Girl!

An ecstatic Tom Cruise and Katie Holmes welcome baby Suri, 7 lbs. 7oz.

At Home with Baby Barron

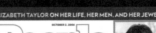

D1314391

JUNE 5, 2006

People

EXCLUSIVE!

A Peterson Juror MY LETTERS FROM SCOTT

KATIE COURIC Her Best & Worst Moments

BEYONCE'S Hot New Body

ELIZABETH TAYLOR ON HER LIFE, HER MEN, AND HER JEWELS

OCTOBER 2, 2006

People

THE ANNA NICOLE SMITH TRAGEDY

HER SON'S FINAL HOURS

• THE SCENE IN THE HOSPITAL ROOM
• THE LATEST ON THE INVESTIGATION
• DANIEL AND ANNA: THEIR SPECIAL BOND

EXCLUSIVE CLAY OPENS UP! About the Gay Rumors, His Panic Attacks And His New Album

KATE BOSWORTH Shockingly Thin

MAY 22, 2006

People

FACING HER POST-PARTUM FEARS

TORI'S SECRET WEDDING

BROOKE SHIELDS New Baby! The actress welcomes little Grier—and talks about the months ahead

BRITNEY'S Pregnant Again

KATIE'S BODY AFTER BABY!

Saint-Tropez: Pamela Anderson and Kid Rock arrive at their wedding reception.

People
THE BEST & WORST OF THE YEAR
YEARBOOK 2007

Taylor Hicks sings his *Idol* best.

2006 CONTENTS

62

76

44

30

EDITOR Cutler Durkee **CREATIVE DIRECTOR** Rina Migliaccio **PHOTOGRAPHY DIRECTOR** Chris Dougherty **DESIGN DIRECTOR** Philip Bratter **ART DIRECTOR** Heather Haggerty **SENIOR EDITOR** Larry Sutton **DESIGNERS** Heath Brockwell, Jorge Colombo **PHOTOGRAPHY EDITOR** Sarah Weissman **WRITERS** Steve Dougherty, Rennie Dyball, Daniel Levy, Mike Neill, Chris Strauss, Charlotte Triggs **REPORTERS** Ansley Roan (Chief), Greg Adkins, David Cobb Craig, Laura Downey, Deirdre Gallagher, Katy Hall, Molly Lopez, Hugh McCarten, Lesley Messer, John Perra, Beth Perry, Ellen Shapiro, Jane Sugden, Christina Tapper, Melody Wells, Marisa Wong, Jennifer Wren **COPY EDITORS** Ben Harte, Rose Kaplan, Alan Levine, Mary Radich **PRODUCTION ARTISTS** Michael Aponte, Denise Doran, Ivy Lee, Michelle Lockhart, Cynthia Miele, Daniel Neuburger, Tracy Whang, Ben Zapp **SCANNERS** Brien Foy, Stephen Pabarue **INTERNS** Jessica Lane, Paul Chi **SPECIAL THANKS TO** Robert Britton, David Barbee, Jane Bealer, Romeo Cifelli, Sal Covarrubias, Francis Fitzgerald, Margery Frohlinger, Charles Guardino, Jeff Ingledue, Charles Nelson, Peter Nora, Ean Sheehy, Jack Styczynski, Celine Wojtala, Patrick Yang

TIME INC. HOME ENTERTAINMENT PUBLISHER Richard Fraiman **EXECUTIVE DIRECTOR, MARKETING SERVICES** Carol Pittard **DIRECTOR, RETAIL & SPECIAL SALES** Tom Mifsud **MARKETING DIRECTOR, BRANDED BUSINESSES** Swati Rao **DIRECTOR, NEW PRODUCT DEVELOPMENT** Peter Harper **FINANCIAL DIRECTOR** Steven Sandonato **ASSISTANT GENERAL COUNSEL** Dasha Smith Dwin **BRAND MANAGER** Laura Adam **BOOK PRODUCTION MANAGER** Suzanne Janso **DESIGN & PREPRESS MANAGER** Anne-Michelle Gallero **SPECIAL THANKS TO** Bozena Bannett, Alexandra Bliss, Glenn Buonocore, Robert Marasco, Brooke McGuire, Jonathan Polsky, Chavaughn Raines, Mary Sarro-Waite, Ilene Schreider, Adriana Tierno

THOMAS ANDERSON, 39

ALVA BENNETT, 51

JIM BENNETT, 61

JERRY GROVES, 56

GEORGE HAMNER JR., 54

TERRY HELMS, 50

JESSE JONES, 44

DAVID LEWIS, 28

MARTIN TOLER JR., 51

FRED WARE JR., 58

JACK WEAVER, 51

MARSHALL WINANS, 50

On the mend and mourning the friends he lost, Sago survivor Randy McCloy wrote their families of their courage and abiding love in the face of death

THE SURVIVOR

"It wasn't bad," one trapped miner scrawled in a note to his family shortly before losing consciousness. "[I] just went to sleep."

THE REACTION

The victims' loved ones struggled to grasp what had happened. "Why can't someone tell us why they did this to our families?" cried one. It was hard to find anyone in the region whose life wasn't touched. Memorials like that above and a permanent one (right) commemorated the disaster. A girl said of her schoolmates: "One lost her father, another his grandfather and another an uncle."

The 13-member crew that began their shift deep in the Sago Mine that day were more than friends, one miner's wife said: "They were actually family underneath there." Said another: "They watched each other's backs."

When disaster struck the family of men below ground, they did just that. Trapped in an airless chamber after an explosion ripped through the Tallmansville, W. Va., mine on Jan. 2, the crew comforted one another and prayed together. When one's emergency air pack failed, another helped him breathe. As rescue teams worked around the clock and families and friends kept vigil in the local Baptist church, the miners slowly ran out of oxygen as their emergency air packs, good for six hours at most, began to fail. "We were worried and afraid, but we began to accept our fate," wrote the lone survivor, Randal McCloy Jr., 27, in a letter to his crewmates' families four months later. "We prayed a little longer, then someone suggested that we each write letters to our loved ones."

Hope was dwindling above as well. Then, near midnight on the second day, word came from the mine that the miners had been rescued. Church bells chimed and families rejoiced at their answered prayers: "They're alive!"

Three hours later came the bewildering, crushing truth: There had been a terrible mistake, a miscommunication between rescue workers and the command center. The 12 reported survivors were, in fact, dead. The only miner found alive, McCloy, was rushed to a trauma center in Morgantown and put on a respirator, with little hope of recovery.

Solace of sorts came with the news that the men did not suffer terribly. "There is no gasping for breath, no choking," an expert in carbon monoxide poisoning said. "Mercifully," he added, the miners would have slowly "drifted into unconsciousness."

Released from the hospital in March, McCloy, whose recovery from carbon monoxide poisoning after 41 hours in the mine astonished most doctors, provided the tragedy's lone glimmer of light. "Things happened that I'd rather I didn't see," McCloy told *Today*'s Matt Lauer. "But I did."

"He had a heart as big as the sky," a victim's sister said as the community of mining families grieved.

"He's like Tarzan meets Indiana Jones," wife Terri said of Irwin (at Australia's Ayers Rock). They first met when she visited his zoo in 1991 and wed nine months later.

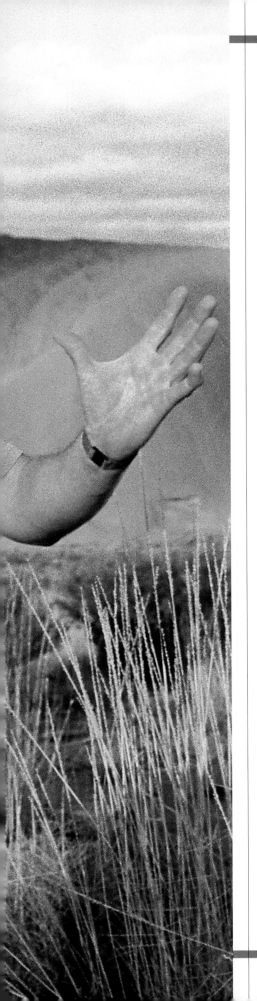

"I don't want Daddy's passion to ever end," Bindi said at Irwin's Sept. 20 memorial. "When I see a crocodile, I will always think of him."

STEVE IRWIN

A FATAL BARB FROM A STINGRAY STRUCK A BELOVED TV CHARACTER—AND MILLIONS OF FANS—IN THE HEART

As Animal Planet's *Crocodile Hunter,* he tussled with killer crocs and all manner of deadly beasts—not to display his bravado, he said, but to educate. And he was beloved as much for his boyish "Crikey!" enthusiasm and his empathy for all earth's wildlife as for his daring. When a stingray's razor-sharp barb struck him in the heart Sept. 4 as he filmed a segment for his 8-year-old daughter Bindi's own planned wildlife show, Irwin, 44, was mourned by fans the world over. In Australia his American-born wife, Terri, Bindi and her little brother Bob, 2, attended a public memorial along with more than 5,000 people at the Australia Zoo he founded for endangered animals. "We've all lost a friend," said actor Russell Crowe. "We've all lost a champion."

With Terri too distraught to speak at the memorial, daughter Bindi read a heartbreaking speech she wrote for her father. "My daddy was my hero," said Bindi, whose Discovery Kids show *Bindi, the Jungle Girl* will air next year. "I want to help endangered wildlife just like he did."

WAR NEWS

SEVERELY WOUNDED BY A ROADSIDE BOMB, ABC'S COANCHOR BECAME A STORY

Just before suffering the wounds that required him to be flown home (below), Woodruff spoke with soldiers in Iraq Jan. 29 (above). Now Woodruff (at home, right) is planning to return to his coanchor chair next spring.

Far from the safe and friendly confines of his New York City broadcast studio, newly promoted ABC *World News Tonight* coanchor Bob Woodruff was riding at the head of a military convoy in Iraq when a roadside bomb—one of the grisly and deadly devices that help make this war peculiarly hellish, accounting for many of the nearly 3,000 American soldiers killed so far—detonated near his vehicle. The blast fractured his skull and shoulder, broke several bones and knocked him unconscious. Wearing a protective vest and helmet, he briefly opened his eyes and asked, "Am I alive?" He was, but barely. Airlifted, along with his less severely injured cameraman Doug Vogt, 46, first to a U.S. military hospital in Germany, then to another in Bethesda, Md., Woodruff had a good chance of surviving, doctors said, but faced untold months of hospitalization and rehabilitation. No one dared predict when, or if, he would return home, much less resume his work. By April, however, he was healing at home in Westchester County, N.Y., where he and his wife, along with their two older children, celebrated their twin daughters' 6th birthday. "It was great to have Bob home for their birthdays," said his wife, Lee. "It was great to have him *alive* for their birthdays."

Struck by Cheney's errant shot, Whittington (below) called the incident a "cloud of misfortune and sadness that is not easy to explain."

MISFIRE!

A TEXAS SHOOTING PARTY PROVES EMBARRASSING FOR DICK CHENEY—AND LIFE-THREATENING FOR A FRIEND

He was supposed to be hunting quail, but on Feb. 11, Vice President Dick Cheney accidentally shot Austin attorney Harry Whittington on a private ranch in Texas. As many as 200 pieces of bird shot struck Whittington in the face, neck and chest. He also suffered a minor heart attack. Critics complained that the White House delayed

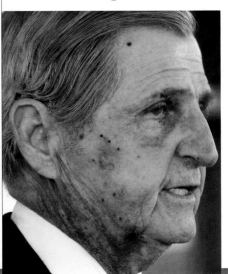

making the news public, and pundits painted the Veep as "trigger happy." Whittington was sorry for the criticism Cheney encountered. Said Cheney of the accident: "It was one of the worst days of my life."

Promoting—yep—*M:i:III* in Los Angeles, Cruise and Holmes self-snapped on the red carpet.

CRUISE'S WILD, WILD RIDE

HE'S UP! HE'S DOWN! HE'S DISSED! HE'S A DAD! HE'S APOLOGIZING! HE'S MARRIED!

No question, Tom Cruise made headlines in 2006. Despite manic promotion, *Mission: Impossible III* took in "only" $400 million. Paramount's Sumner Redstone blamed the shortfall on Cruise's couch-jumping antics and other behavior—"He turned off all women.... He was embarrassing the studio"— and didn't renew his contract. On a more positive note, Cruise personally apologized to Brooke Shields for criticizing her use of drugs to battle postpartum depression; celebrated, with Katie Holmes, the birth of daughter Suri; partnered with a new studio, United Artists— and wed Holmes in Italy on Nov. 18.

In Mexico a bemused Cruise posed with a pack of paparazzi at the local *M:i:III* premiere.

VanRyn (below) died in the crash; her friend Cerak (right) suffered major injuries.

TRAGIC ERROR

A CRUEL MIX-UP CAUSES A HEARTBREAKING DANCE BETWEEN GRIEF AND JOY

A 22-year-old woman believed to be Taylor University senior Laura VanRyn lay in a coma for five weeks following a horrific highway accident April 26 in Indiana. VanRyn's family kept vigil at her bedside and posted pleas on their blog to "please pray for her to emerge from her coma soon." When she did, the VanRyns received an unfathomable shock: "The young woman we have been taking care of . . . has not been our dear Laura." She was Whitney Cerak, 19, a Taylor freshman. VanRyn, her near look-alike, had been buried in her place. Said VanRyn's boyfriend: "I felt like it's the biggest trick [God]'s ever played on me."

HOW COULD IT HAPPEN?
A coroner's original misidentification of one of five accident fatalities and a severely injured survivor was compounded when the family of the actual survivor, Cerak, decided on a closed casket. Inside was her look-alike schoolmate, VanRyn.

VERY BAD BREAK

AFTER A ROUSING WIN IN THE KENTUCKY DERBY, TRIPLE CROWN FAVORITE BARBARO SEVERELY INJURES HIS ANKLE

American Thoroughbred Barbaro sustained life-threatening injuries when he broke his right rear ankle in three places just steps into the Preakness Stakes on May 20 in Baltimore. His racing career ruined, the 1,200-lb. Kentucky Derby winner endured a five-hour operation to insert 27 screws and later underwent more surgery to battle infection. Although the steed was forced to retire, his once dim prospects for survival—he was given only a 50 percent chance at one point—are brighter, and breeders say he's got a great career ahead as a stud.

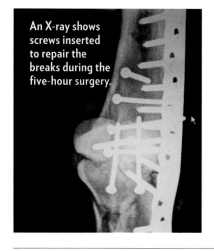

An X-ray shows screws inserted to repair the breaks during the five-hour surgery.

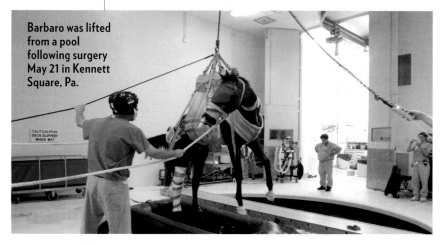

Barbaro was lifted from a pool following surgery May 21 in Kennett Square, Pa.

Jockey Edgar Prado tried to steady Barbaro after he suffered the agonizing break at Pimlico Race Course in Baltimore.

MEL GIBSON

AFTER A NIGHT OF DRINKING, THE OSCAR WINNER LAUNCHED INTO AN UGLY TIRADE, THREATENING HIS CAREER AND HIS IMAGE

It's not every day that bar patrons get to bend elbows with a bona fide movie star. But there was Mel Gibson, vodka bottle in hand, partying with perfect strangers at Malibu's beachside Moonshadows bar July 27. "He wasn't falling down drunk," recalled a guest of her new-found drinking buddy, "but the kind of tipsy where you just want to love everyone."

Hours later, when Gibson, 50, was pulled over in his 2006 Lexus after hitting 87 mph in a 45-mph zone on Pacific Coast Highway, he was certifiably drunk—and anything but loveable. "F------ Jews," he yelled at the arresting officer, who happened to be Jewish. "The Jews are responsible for all the wars in the world. Are you a Jew?"

When his words were made public the next day, Gibson, dogged by accusations of anti-Semitism after some critics said his 2004 blockbuster *The Passion of the Christ* blamed Jews for killing Jesus, faced a ferocious backlash from both the public and his peers. "His career is over," said one Hollywood executive. "He's going to become toxic." ABC quickly canceled plans for a miniseries about the Holocaust that Gibson was set to produce.

Gibson began rehab within days of the incident and issued not one but two apologies. "I am deeply ashamed," he said, and later thanked the arresting officer, James Mee, for "probably saving me from myself."

"I like that he apologized," a friend said of Gibson, who was sentenced to three years' probation on Aug. 17. "And now he has to mean it."

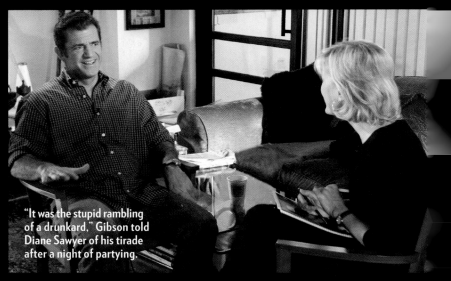

"It was the stupid rambling of a drunkard," Gibson told Diane Sawyer of his tirade after a night of partying.

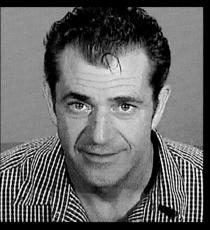

Mugging with bar patrons, and for the police (left).

At Moonshadows Gibson amiably posed for cell phone photos and poured drinks.

"The whole building shook," an eyewitness told *The New York Times*.

HIGH-RISE HELL

A BIZARRE PLANE CRASH CREATES A TOWERING INFERNO, TAKING THE LIFE OF NEW YORK YANKEES PITCHER CORY LIDLE

For New Yorkers, the news brought back unsettling memories of 9/11: A plane had slammed into a 50-story building on Manhattan's Upper East Side. But the Oct. 11 crash turned out to be tragedy, not terrorism, taking the lives of New York Yankees pitcher Cory Lidle, 34, and his flying instructor, Tyler Stranger, 26. Authorities concluded the plane, attempting an extremely tight turn, had been pushed off course by the wind.

FACE TO FACE

 + =

AFTER RECEIVING THE WORLD'S FIRST FACE TRANSPLANT, ISABELLE DINOIRE IS CHASTISED FOR RISKING ITS SUCCESS

After a horrific dog attack disfigured her, Dinoire, 39, made history when French doctors grafted the nose, lips and chin of Maryline Saint-Aubert (above right, as a teenager), a 46-year-old schoolteacher who had died shortly before the surgery in November 2005. Barely two months later, Dinoire (above left, and right) was widely criticized for chain-smoking cigarettes, which could cause her body to reject the transplant. "[Smoking is] not the best new thing she's started doing," said one of her surgeons. "But if that's what she wants to do, we can't stop her."

DAVID BLAINE

THE HUMAN GOLDFISH DREW HUGE CROWDS. BUT SETTING A RECORD? ALAS, DON'T HOLD YOUR BREATH

Blaine remained in this water-filled sphere for a little more than seven days.

So close! Magician David Blaine had a grand idea: break the world record for holding one's breath underwater, during a weeklong stint inside a Plexiglas bubble at New York City's Lincoln Center. But after 177 hours in the tank, living off Pedialyte (an infant formula that replaces lost fluids), Gatorade and oxygen tubes, Blaine, 33, lasted only 7 minutes and 8 seconds without air, missing the record by about 2 minutes. The televised event scored okay ratings for ABC, but Blaine was hospitalized for partial liver and kidney failure. He also suffered from rashes and loss of sensation in his hands and feet. And really wrinkled skin.

Triumph to tears: He took a victory lap on July 23, then faced the press July 28 (below).

FLOYD LANDIS

BANISHED FROM HIS CYCLING TEAM AND HIS TITLE IN JEOPARDY AFTER TESTING POSITIVE FOR DOPING, HE WANTS HIS DAY IN COURT

As if the three-week, 2,267-mile endurance race wasn't tough enough, he did it with a damaged hip. But the celebration of Landis's come-from-behind win in the Tour de France—fans hailed it as the ride of the century—quickly soured for the 31-year-old pride of Farmersville, Pa. In a fall from grace far more painful than any spill he ever took from a bike, Landis was accused of cheating after tests appeared to

confirm that he had used synthetic testosterone. Vehemently denying guilt and seeking to prove he was misdiagnosed, Landis knows that even if his title is confirmed, damage done to his name may be beyond repair. "Unfortunately," he told TIME, "I don't think it's ever going to go away."

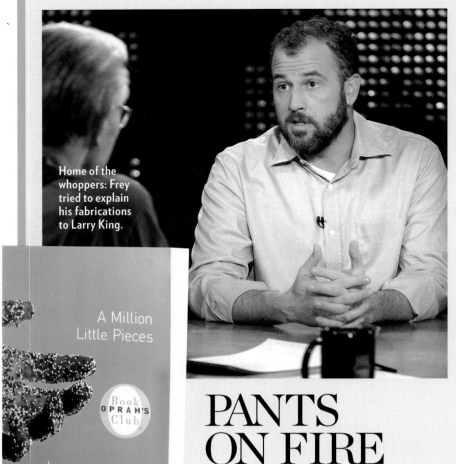

Home of the whoppers: Frey tried to explain his fabrications to Larry King.

A Million Little Pieces

Book OPRAH'S Club

James Frey

PANTS ON FIRE

AFTER FABRICATING PARTS OF HIS MEMOIR, JAMES FREY LOST HIS AGENT AND A POWERFUL ALLY: OPRAH WINFREY

A Million Little Pieces, James Frey's breathless, *muy macho* 2003 account of drug addiction and recovery, became a runaway hit after Oprah Winfrey called it "raw and real" and said she "couldn't put it down." There was, alas, one problem: On Jan. 9, after a painstaking survey of court records and interviews with cops, thesmokinggun.com revealed that many of *Pieces'* key details—from Frey's alleged crack-fueled run-in with an Ohio police officer in 1992 to his involvement in a friend's fatal car accident—were pure hokum. Outraged, an avenging Oprah laid waste to Frey, 37, and his editor, Nan Talese, on live TV—and Random House offered refunds to buyers with a proof of purchase.

YEP, HE'S GAY

LANCE BASS CAME OUT: "I'M MORE LIBERATED AND HAPPY THAN I'VE EVER BEEN"

With gossip blogs questioning his "friendship" with openly gay *Amazing Race* winner Reichen Lehmkuhl, Bass, 27, decided to share his secret with his family. "It was very hard," he says. "It really does hurt knowing that they're going to have to live with this back home [in Clinton, Miss.] in a place where it's not looked at very highly." Even so, "they took it so well," says Bass, who eventually told some of his former 'N Sync bandmates. "I told Joey Fatone, and he was like, 'Dude, I don't care,'" says Bass. Now, with a sitcom in the works and a stable relationship with Lehmkuhl, 32, Bass is "taking it one day at a time" and is, he says, "at peace with my family, my friends, myself and God—there's really nothing else I can worry about."

"I've known my whole life," says Bass (right, with Lehmkuhl). "It's nothing that was confusing to me."

NATASCHA KAMPUSCH

HELD CAPTIVE FOR ALMOST HALF HER LIFE IN AN UNDERGROUND BUNKER, A TEENAGE GIRL STRUGGLES TO FIND HER WAY IN FREEDOM'S UNFAMILIAR TERRAIN

Her nightmare—and her parents'—began on March 2, 1998, when she was 10 years old. That's when Wolfgang Priklopil, a 36-year-old telecom technician, yanked Kampusch into his minibus as she walked to school. For eight years, he kept her prisoner in a hidden 6-ft.-by-10-ft. basement room in his house in Strasshof, Austria, 10 miles from her Vienna home. When she was 12, she said, "I made a pact with my future self that the day would come when that 12-year-old girl would be freed." That day came in August, when she made a daring escape, dashing from Priklopil's garage as he took a cell-phone call. "I climbed over the fences . . . in a panic, like in an action film," she said. Now 18, Kampusch has found adjustment to life outside her prison difficult. Her parents divorced before she was abducted, and her reunion with them was tense. "I felt a little overwhelmed and a little cramped," she said. And she is, she said, "in a way, mourning" Priklopil, who committed suicide after her escape. Still, she says, "I am overcome by the thought of freedom."

"I dreamt of chopping his head off," says Kampusch (above) of her abductor Priklopil (below). Life in her cell (left), she said, consisted of "housework, reading, television, talking, cooking. That's all there was, year in and year out."

IN THE SPOT

LEGALLY SINGLE AGAIN, *THE BREAK-UP* STAR TRIES TO BALANCE A PUBLIC CAREER AND A PRIVATE LIFE

The year after her split from Brad Pitt, pop culture's It Girl went on rebuilding her life. Professionally, her move to film continued to be a work in progress: 2005's *Rumor Has It . . .* and *Friends with Money,* in 2006, disappointed at the box office, but *The Break-Up* earned about $118 million. Famously, it also brought her another perk: Aniston and costar Vince Vaughn became involved while filming in the summer of 2005. "They met at a time when she needed someone to make her smile," a friend of Vaughn's said. "Now it's evolved into a true love affair."

One that tabloids viewed much the way sugar-hyped children view a low-hanging piñata: In any given week the actress could read that she was engaged, broken up or pregnant. Aniston ignored the talk until reports of an imminent marriage surfaced on usually reliable news shows, then spoke out. "When [the gossip] starts to travel into the *Today* show, CNN, then you go, 'This is insane!' The thing that got me was that I was getting phone calls from Greece! My Aunt Mary in Greece is getting accused of lying!" For the record, she said, "I'm not engaged, and I haven't been proposed to." She and Vaughn were fine, she said, "just being."

LIGHT

Rumors that Aniston (left, in October) and Vaughn (in June) were turning their flick *The Break-Up* into reality were, said pal David Arquette, "complete horse doo-doo."

THE RUMOR RUMBA:
DANCE OF MODERN MEDIA

1. JEN DENIES ENGAGEMENT In August, amid reports that Vaughn had proposed on bended knee, Aniston set the record straight to PEOPLE: "I'm not engaged."

2. APART Vaughn went to London to film *Fred Claus*; Aniston chilled at home in Malibu, walking her dogs and hanging with pals Courteney Cox Arquette and yoga instructor Mandy Ingber. The distance sparks talk of a split.

3. MYSTERY BLONDE British tabloids breathlessly claim Vaughn smooched another woman in London. Mystery solved: He was giving a g'night peck to producer Kate Pakenham, in whose *24 Hour Plays* benefit he appeared. The reaction "has been a bit crazy," the happily married Pakenham told PEOPLE.

4. JEN DISHES As split gossip gains momentum, Aniston tells Oprah Oct. 16 that they're still a couple. A real-life *Break-Up*? "No, no," says Aniston.

Castro (after a 1960 TV appearance) became Cuba's youngest-ever prime minister when a 1959 military coup put him in power at age 32.

FIDEL CASTRO

IN THE AUTUMN OF THE PATRIARCH, CUBA'S STRONGMAN STEPS BACK

He has survived history—and outlasted nine United States Presidents—to become the world's longest-ruling strongman. But in 2006, it seemed as if mortality might finally be catching up with Cuba's leader. After more than 45 years in power, Castro, 80, temporarily stepped down after surgery for gastrointestinal bleeding. Handing over the presidency to his charisma-challenged brother Raul, 75, Castro explained that stress "caused in me an acute intestinal crisis." In a message to the nation, read by his secretary on TV July 31, he added, "The operation will force me to undertake several weeks of rest." Those several weeks turned into months, though, and Castro didn't show up to meet Russian prime minister Mikhail Fradkov when he visited Cuba in late September. In October brother Raul had to deny rumors that Fidel was terminally ill. "He is not dying," he said. "He is constantly getting better."

NOT YOUR MOTHER'S GRAPE BOYCOTT

JAY-Z LEADS A PROTEST AGAINST A FAVORITE STATUS SYMBOL, CRISTAL. SO WHAT'S NEXT—HIP HOPS?

Cristal, the $300 champagne, got props in many rap songs. This did not amuse the bubbly's managing director, Frédéric Rouzaud, who implied the free PR was downscale. "What can we do?" he told *The Economist*. "We can't forbid people from buying it." He may not have to fret. Rapper Jay-Z stopped selling Cristal in his clubs and called for a boycott. He also plans to rewrite Cristal lyrics in his old songs. What rhymes with Dom Pérignon?

QUITTIN' TIME

BROKEBACK MOUNTAIN FINDS AN AUDIENCE—AND OSCARS

A mainstream movie about cowboys in love? Director Ang Lee took a risk and was rewarded: The film, starring Heath Ledger and Jake Gyllenhaal as ranch hands who love each other more than their wives, received eight Oscar nominations (and won three, including best director), earned more than $80 million at the box office and added at least one phrase to the language: "I wish I knew how to quit you."

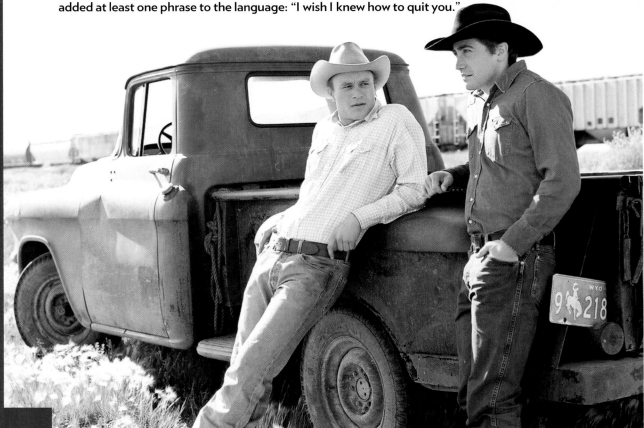

After a lifetime of giving, Astor (above) was taken by her son (below), says *his* son.

HEIR RAID

DUNNED DOWAGER? BROOKE ASTOR'S GRANDSON ACCUSES HIS FATHER OF MISTREATING A GREAT DAME AND LOOTING HER ESTATE

The clinking of ice cubes on crystal and the crack of croquet mallets were not the only sounds heard at the lawn parties of the very, very rich last summer. The haves buzzed about the tribulations of the bluest blood of all, the most upper of all the crust, Brooke Astor, the 104-year-old philanthropist, socialite and heir-by-marriage to the John Jacob Astor fortune. Brooke's care, and her $45 million estate, became the center of an ugly legal battle between her only son, Anthony, 82, and her grandson Philip Marshall, 53, who filed court papers alleging his father had neglected Brooke "while enriching himself with millions of dollars." The allegations—

that he and his wife, Charlene, fired her staff and made her sleep in a torn nightgown on a sofa in her Park Avenue duplex—created a grist storm at the gossip mill. In response, authorities removed Brooke from Anthony's custody and installed a friend as temporary guardian. At Holly Hill, her 75-acre New York estate, Brooke, said her grandson, was "eating well, feeling much better and very happy to be home." In October, as part of a settlement, Anthony agreed to step aside as caretaker and repay more than $1 million to the estate.

"He was happy," a friend said of Daniel, with his newborn sister shortly before he died.

ANNA NICOLE SMITH

IN THE SPACE OF A FEW DAYS SHE HAD A BABY AND LOST A SON; THEN SHE CELEBRATED A LONGTIME LOVE

It was a painfully whipsaw year for Anna Nicole Smith. First came good news from the Supreme Court, which ruled she could pursue her claim to her late oilman husband J. Howard Marshall II's $1.6 billion fortune. Next arrived joy with the Sept. 7 birth of daughter Dannielynn. Then came the unthinkable: Son Daniel, 20, who had flown to the Bahamas to visit his mother and infant sister, died from a lethal combination of prescription drugs. Some solace came Sept. 28 when Smith and her lawyer Howard K. Stern, who said on *Larry King Live* that he was the baby's father, declared their love in a ceremony off the coast of Paradise Island. "Howard and Anna were both crying and kissing and holding hands," said a friend. "It was kind of sad and happy at the same time."

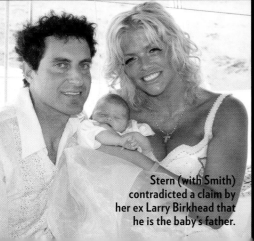

Stern (with Smith) contradicted a claim by her ex Larry Birkhead that he is the baby's father.

Things seemed to be going swimmingly for Smith and her beau Stern after their Sept. 28 non-wedding ceremony on a beach in the Bahamas.

TOMATO COUP

"I woke up and I'm like, 'Did that really happen?'" White said of the morning after his gold-medal-winning performance.

FLAME-HAIRED SNOWBOARDER SHAUN WHITE—THE FLYING TOMATO—TOOK THE TURIN OLYMPICS BY SOAR

Stoked as he was during the awards ceremony Feb. 12, when he received the gold medal for his gravity-defying performance in the Olympic halfpipe snowboarding competition, Shaun White—a.k.a. the Flying Tomato—got teary. "I looked over and the whole family is doing the sob," White, now 20, said of his parents, brother and sister, who'd flown from their home in Big Bear, Calif., to cheer the hero dude. "I shed a couple of tears. It was cool." Despite the adulation—and more than $1 million in endorsement deals—"he's still the same kid, goofing off, having fun," said his brother. "He's just superchill."

Flying, Tomato style:
As an infant he survived two heart surgeries. "They almost lost me," he said.

GOOD & EVIL

Slaughter of innocents:
A gunman's attack on children
in a Pennsylvania schoolhouse
shocked the nation—and
revealed the amazing faith and
forgiveness of the Amish

State Police
Commissioner Jeffrey
Miller displayed
the killer's checklist
for the attack.

"He was a nice guy, very nice," an Amish man said of Roberts (in an undated photo above). After the attack, his body was removed from the schoolhouse (top right); a horse-and-buggy procession carried mourners to a cemetery Oct. 5 (top left).

The crime, like the bloody scene at the out-of-time one-room Amish schoolhouse, was impossible to comprehend. Ten young girls, ages 6 to 13, dressed identically in prim dresses and aprons, their ankles bound, shot in the back at point-blank range by a gunman who was also their neighbor. When it was over, four of the girls lay dead and a fifth mortally wounded; five others were hospitalized in critical condition. The killer, a milk-truck driver named Charlie Roberts, 32, shot himself as police stormed the schoolhouse. In a cell-phone call to his wife shortly before he died, he hinted that he was tormented by the urge to molest children; in a suicide note, he said he was "filled with so much hate"—perhaps stemming from the 1997 death of a prematurely born daughter. It made sense to no one. "I just can't see why that man thought he had to do this," said 14-year-old Raymond Stoltzfus, whose sister Rachel Ann, 8, was one of the wounded survivors. "Did he know what he was doing, or what?"

The attack shattered the tranquility of the Amish community that thrives in Nickel Mines, Pa., and the surrounding area. "They are stoic," said a local with close ties to the Amish, who live without modern conveniences such as electricity and automobiles and who are much respected for their piety and peaceful way of life. "But we fell into each other's arms and cried. They're as human as anyone else."

And almost superhuman in their capacity to forgive: Even as they buried their innocents, families of the victims reached out to the family of the murderer, offering prayers for Roberts and his own wife and children. "They said the Roberts family has a greater load to bear than the Amish families," a nurse who helped deliver two of the victims said, "because not only must they bear grief for losing the shooter, but also the shame and guilt."

PREACHER'S WIFE

PARISHIONERS WONDER WHAT LED A POPULAR PREACHER'S WIFE TO MURDER HER HUSBAND

"I can't imagine her harming a bug," a friend said of Mary (in Alabama).

Mary and Matthew with Brianna, Mary Alice and Patricia in an undated photo.

To members of his tight-knit congregation, pastor Matthew Winkler and his wife, Mary, seemed the ideal couple. "What struck everyone about them," said one member of the Fourth Street Church of Christ in Selmer, Tenn., "was how close they were and the love they showed for each other. They seemed to be a loving, devoted family."

That happy portrait was shattered Wednesday, March 22, when the pastor was found lying faceup in bed, dead from a shotgun wound to the back. Mary, with the couple's three daughters in tow, was arrested the next day after her minivan was stopped by police in Orange Beach, Ala., 390 miles away. When Matthew's parents, who were assigned temporary custody of their grandchildren (Patricia, 8, Mary Alice, 6 and 1-year-old Brianna) visited Mary in jail the day after her arrest, "they told her, 'We forgive you for what you did,'" a family friend said. But in June when a grand jury indicted her for first-degree murder, which could bring the death penalty, her lawyer hinted that he might argue that she had been the victim of spousal abuse. Matthew's family strongly denied the charge. "There was zero of that—zero," said a friend of the family. "Some people feel sorry for her," said another friend of the family. "But she had a choice. I would imagine if my husband was emotionally abusive, before I'd kill him, I'd just leave."

The Entwistles (in 2005) moved to their new home weeks before the murders.

BOSTON HEARTBREAK

AUTHORITIES SAY NEIL ENTWISTLE, FACING A FINANCIAL CRISIS, MURDERED HIS WIFE AND BABY DAUGHTER AND FLED TO ENGLAND

DNA evidence led prosecutors to charge Entwistle with double murder Feb. 16.

The horrific crime scene made national headlines: a mother, Rachel Entwistle, 27, and her infant daughter, Lillian, found shot dead in bed together in their suburban Boston home. The day before, her husband, Neil, also 27, grabbed a flight to his native England, where he remained on Feb. 1 when mother and daughter were buried. A prime suspect, Neil returned to the U.S. and was charged with two counts of first-degree murder; his trial is expected to begin next April. Prosecutors said he was beset by debt, some incurred from failed pornographic Web ventures.

Fires that damaged one sanctuary (above) and burned another to its foundations (below) were like "murder," a parishioner said.

FEAR, FLAMES AND FAITH

CHURCH FIRES SPREAD FEAR IN THE SOUTH; COPS BELIEVE THREE COLLEGE KIDS DID IT FOR KICKS

In eight days in February, 10 Baptist churches in rural Bibb County, Ala., fell victim to arson, prompting headlines and a massive investigation. In an area where church burnings can ignite terrible memories, fears that the fires were racially motivated were dampened by the fact that both black and white churches were targeted. Even so, there was relief a month later when authorities arrested three college students, who face up to five years in prison for each church they allegedly torched if convicted. All three have pleaded not guilty. "The fire that's waiting for them," a man said, "is a whole lot hotter than the ones they set."

FACING 50 YEARS EACH IF CONVICTED

"This is not a hate crime," said an FBI special agent. According to authorities, Russell Lee DeBusk Jr., 19 (left), Matthew Lee Cloyd, 20 (center), and Benjamin Nathan Moseley, 19, did it for fun. "They were excited by the fact there were fires." Unknowingly "they did us a favor," said a member of a burned black church after praying in a nearby white church for the first time. "Because they brought people together."

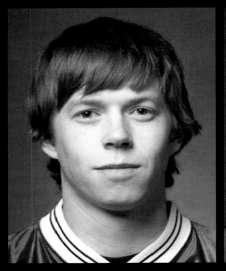

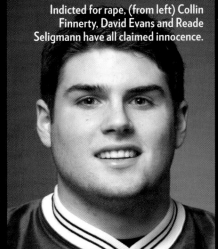

Indicted for rape, (from left) Collin Finnerty, David Evans and Reade Seligmann have all claimed innocence.

DUKE DRAMA

A CONTROVERSIAL RAPE CASE IGNITES SIMMERING TENSIONS ON AN IDYLLIC CAMPUS

In a powder-keg racial case, three white members of Duke University's lacrosse team were accused of raping a black 27-year-old mother of two who had been hired as a stripper at an off-campus party March 13. Serious questions about the evidence—and the fact that a second stripper at the scene called the charges a "crock"—in turn led some to publicly wonder whether Durham County D.A. Mike Nifong was exploiting the case to enhance his reelection campaign. (He won.) A trial is expected next spring.

Protestors gathered at the site of the alleged sexual assault in Durham, N.C., in April.

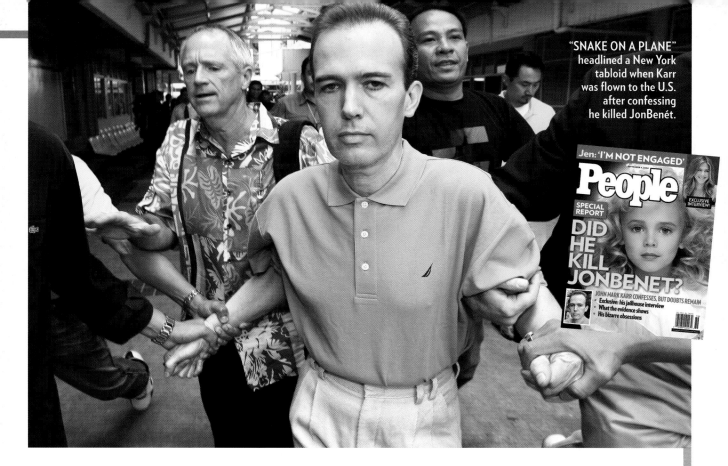

"SNAKE ON A PLANE" headlined a New York tabloid when Karr was flown to the U.S. after confessing he killed JonBenét.

Jen: 'I'M NOT ENGAGED'

People

SPECIAL REPORT

DID HE KILL JONBENET?

JOHN MARK KARR CONFESSES, BUT DOUBTS REMAIN
- Exclusive: his jailhouse interview
- What the evidence shows
- His bizarre obsessions

NEVER MIND

A NIGHTMARISHLY ODD TEACHER CLAIMED HE KILLED JONBENET

Tiny beauty queen JonBenét Ramsey's body was discovered in her family home on the day after Christmas, 1996, yet—despite tremendous effort and expense—no official suspect had ever been named in her murder. That changed spectacularly on Aug. 16 when Bangkok police detained a suspect who claimed to be the killer. Looking like a creepy cross between Lee Harvey Oswald and Mr. Rogers, John Mark Karr, 41, a teacher and fugitive from child-porn charges in California, had been fired from a succession of schools for inappropriate behavior. He had carried on a correspondence with the imprisoned killer of 12-year-old Polly Klaas and even moved to Klaas's hometown. In the end his "confession" proved as reliable as screening procedures of the many schools that had hired him. Why the obviously delusional Karr perpetuated the macabre hoax— and why Boulder County's district attorney had let the case against him proceed so far before abruptly releasing him—added further layers of mystery to a sad and bewildering crime.

A FITFUL PEACE
Once said by authorities to be under an "umbrella of suspicion," along with her husband, John, Patsy Ramsey (visiting JonBenét's grave in 2001) learned of a supposed break in the case shortly before she died of ovarian cancer, at age 49, in Roswell, Ga., in June.

NIGHT STALKE

SHE COULD HAVE BEEN ANY COLLEGE STUDENT; IMETTE ST. GUILLEN'S DEATH A CHILLING REMINDER OF THE RANDOMNESS OF EVIL

Out for a night of fun in February, 24-year-old graduate student Imette St. Guillen and her friend Claire Higgins hit Manhattan's Pioneer Bar. Higgins decided to call it quits around 2:30 a.m.; St. Guillen headed to another pub, the Falls, by herself. That evening, police found St. Guillen's body rolled up in a blanket near a Brooklyn highway.

She had been strangled and tortured—her hands bound with plastic ties, a sock lodged in her throat, and her face wrapped in packing tape. "You don't see innocent people tortured like this very often," one law enforcement official told PEOPLE. "We're dealing with a very sick, sadistic person."

The case broke when Danny Dorrian, whose family owned the bar, told authorities he had asked bouncer Darryl Littlejohn to escort an inebriated St. Guillen out of the bar at 4 a.m. the night she disappeared. (Dorrian initially withheld that information from police.) Littlejohn, on parole for the armed robbery of a Long Island bank, had an extensive criminal record and only got his job at the bar by claiming to be a federal marshal. Though Littlejohn denied the charges, police say DNA evidence links him to the crime scene. The Falls closed June 9 after city officials called it "a serious public nuisance."

NYS DOCS

00A1792
BLAZE, JONATHAN
5'7"   175lbs
DATE 07/29/2003

THE SUSPECT

A 6 a.m. cell phone call placed Darryl Littlejohn (in mug shot, with alias), a bouncer at the Falls (above) where St. Guillen (inset) was last seen alive, in the area where her body was found.

Samuel Dieteman (left) and Dale Hausner were suspects in arson incidents at Wal-Mart stores. That investigation led to their arrests for the shootings.

DUAL REIGN OF TERROR

THE ARREST OF TWO MEN FOR THE SERIAL SHOOTER KILLINGS DOESN'T END PHOENIX'S NIGHTMARE

Though police arrested a suspect in a sex assault linked to the Baseline Killer in September, the manhunt continues.

It seemed like something out of a very disturbing thriller—not one but two serial killers loose around Phoenix since 2005. The so-called Serial Shooter, who specialized in picking off pedestrians and bicyclists on city streets at night, had killed seven and wounded 18, police said. A fellow predator known as the Baseline Killer is believed to have committed eight murders and a string of rapes and robberies. Together they created a city under siege. Partial relief came Aug. 3 when police arrested two Mesa, Ariz., roommates in connection with the Serial Shooter killings, which one suspect chillingly called "random recreational violence."

BRIDAL SHOW

From Keith and Nicole's Sydney storybook celebration to Pam and Kid's raucous revelry, the couples of 2006 put their own stamp on the institution of marriage

"They're so near and dear to me," said Marcia Cross of the flower girls (her niece and friends' daughters) at her June 24 wedding. "I couldn't think of anything better."

MARCIA CROSS & TOM MAHONEY

THE CAKE
"The entire event just felt like barefoot elegance," said *Desperate Housewives* costar Brenda Strong.

LOVE IN BLOOM: From the heart-shaped peony wreath over the church door, to the cocktail lounge bursting with white tulips, casablancas and calla lilies, to the roses and lilacs layering the wedding cake, flowers were more than just a decoration at the wedding of the *Desperate Housewives* actress, 44, and her money manager beau, 48. The "flower shop" look was a tribute to their first encounter in 2004, when an employee at an L.A. florist offered to pass her number to a handsome stranger in the store. "He called me a week later!" she recalled.

DESPERATE PEOPLE: There were plenty of neighbors from Wisteria Lane at Church of Our Savior Episcopal Parish in San Gabriel, Calif., where *Housewives* pals Eva Longoria, Felicity Huffman, Doug Savant and creator Marc Cherry watched Cross cascade down the aisle in a satin Reem Acra gown and Neil Lane diamonds. The party continued at Pasadena's Ritz-Carlton, where they dined on sea bass and filet mignon.

TIME'S A-WASTIN': Just 2½ months after the wedding, Cross called Cherry with the real-life news that "Bree's pregnant." The couple expect their first child in April 2007.

PAMELA ANDERSON & KID ROCK

REUNION TOUR: Just weeks after restarting their roller-coaster romance, the former fiancés (they split up in 2003) made it to the altar, tying the knot in a five-minute rock and roll shipboard ceremony July 29 in Saint-Tropez.

NOT EXACTLY BLUSHING: After releasing white balloons, Anderson, 39, whipped off her Heatherette minidress to reveal a white bikini underneath, which she'd sport during the wild reception at local restaurant Nikki Beach. Rock, 35, was just as formal, spending most of the night shirtless.

LEGAL, SHMEGAL: Who lets silly regulations stand in the way of love? Since French law requires a prior civil ceremony at the mayor's office plus three months' residency, the marriage wasn't actually official. Not that Anderson cared. "It was the best, most romantic wedding of all time," she posted on her Web site.

THE YACHT
The ceremony took place on the *Altavida*, a $20 million chartered love boat whose name means "high life" in Spanish.

NICOLE KIDMAN & KEITH URBAN

GOOD LIGHTING: Before the bride's arrival, more than 1,000 white candles flickered a welcome to guests. Says one: "It was like you were walking into a fairy tale." Enter the princess: As she marched down the aisle, "spotlights lit Nicole up like this angel," says the guest. "Keith just seemed in awe."

YOU MAY KISS THE BRIDE—*REALLY* KISS HER: To seal the deal after the nearly hour-long ceremony, "Keith gave [Nicole] the longest, most passionate kiss," says another guest. "Everything went from being quiet to really loud, like we were suddenly at a soccer game. We were hooting and hollering for at least a minute. The place erupted."

MUSICAL SELECTIONS: There wasn't a dry eye at the reception as Urban serenaded Kidman with his hit "Making Memories of Us." But the evening wasn't all teary love songs: The 220 guests (among them: Russell Crowe, Hugh Jackman and Naomi Watts, who shared a dance with Kidman's son Connor) looked on as the newlyweds cut loose to the Skyhooks's "You Just Like Me 'Cos I'm Good in Bed."

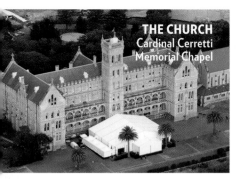

THE CHURCH
Cardinal Cerretti
Memorial Chapel

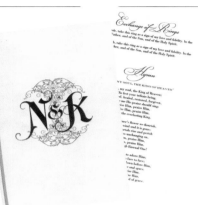

THE BRIDAL PARTY: Kidman's daughter Isabella, 13 (left), niece and flower girl Lucia, 7, and sister Antonia, 35, arrived in a Rolls-Royce matching Kidman's.
TOAST OF THE TOWN: Thousands of well-wishers lined the streets of Sydney as Kidman made her way to the ceremony, moving the actress to tears (and new makeup).
SAIL AWAY: On their French Polynesian honeymoon, the couple didn't have to go far for a dip: Their private villa was situated just a few sandy steps away from the turquoise sea.

"[It was] the best day of my life,"says McDermott. "By far!" adds Spelling. The couple combined Fijian tradition (above) with a ceremony honoring his deceased parents and her childhood nanny. "We had invitations for each of them that we burned in a fire," McDermott says. "I know for a fact that my mom and dad brought Tori into my life."

THE PARTY
Surrounded by locals, the newlyweds take in the full island atmosphere.

TORI SPELLING & DEAN McDERMOTT

ZIP CODE UNKNOWN: With only a nondenominational officiant present, the *90210* star, 33, and her actor husband, 40, opted for a barefoot beachfront ceremony on the private island of Wakaya in Fiji. SO NO-TORI-OUS: After meeting on an Ottawa set in August 2005, the pair (who were both married to others at the time) felt immediate sparks. By New Year's they had both filed for divorce and were engaged to each other. "I feel sorry for people who meet the One and let it pass them by," says Spelling. "We were meant to be together." GOAL!!!!: "We're going to make a baby," forecast McDermott after the wedding. "We want to have nine kids!" Added Spelling: "He likes to play hockey, so we're going to make a hockey team." They've already got their future goalie on the way: A source confirmed in October that they'll be expecting their first child in the spring.

PINK & CAREY HART

PINK LADY: "I transformed into a girl!" joked the tomboyish pop rebel, 27, about her engagement to motocross racer Hart, 31. The couple's elaborate Jan. 7 Costa Rican wedding mixed high extravagance (more than 10,000 roses) and rock and roll (their first dance was to a song from *Natural Born Killers*), with the bride donning a "goth" ivory-and-black Monique Lhuillier gown for the occasion. **PROMISES, PROMISES:** Even Hart's roughneck friends were moved by the newlyweds' handwritten vows, which included gems like her "I see us breaking lots of bones, risking death and bodily injury" and his "You love my crazy family and accept my white trashiness." **RIDDLE SOLVED:** "I was trying to figure out who the heck would marry my daughter," toasted Pink's father, James Moore, at the rehearsal dinner. "And there he is!"

"I wanted to kiss him as soon as I got up there," said Pink. "I'd never seen him in a suit before!" After a tent-covered reception, the pair partied with 140 guests including friend Lisa Marie Presley (below) at the "punk rock and roll nightclub"-themed afterparty at the Four Seasons Resort. "They have a deep appreciation for each other's personalities," said L.A. Reid, who first signed Pink. Added pal Stephen Webster: "They're both crazy in their own way."

L.A. BAKERS
The Cake Divas crafted a "heavy-metal" treat from Duncan Hines batter.

As Priscilla Presley (above) walked her daughter down the aisle, "Michael looked so happy," said planner Kara Keaney. After dinner, the couple cut into the vanilla buttercream dessert (below), which featured the character for congratulations and long life, and visited with three local geisha who performed earlier at the reception. "It was fascinating," says Keaney.

They nixed a first dance but weren't shy about showing affection. "They seemed very happy," said the groom's dad, William Lockwood.

Each course was written in gold calligraphy on menus decorated with a gold, fan-shaped charm.

LISA MARIE PRESLEY & MICHAEL LOCKWOOD

KYOTO ACCORD: For her fourth trip down the aisle, Presley, 37, and music producer Lockwood, 44, opted for an original yet small-scale production at a private inn in Kyoto, Japan. The 16 guests donned custom-fitted kimonos at the sunset ceremony, where the pair, who started dating in 2003 (he also executive-produced Presley's 2005 album *Now What*), performed a Japanese sake ritual after exchanging traditional vows.

RETURN TO SENDER: Never conventional (see, particularly, marriage No. 2, to Michael Jackson), Elvis's daughter shook things up by having Danny Keough, her first husband and father of her kids Riley, 16, and Benjamin, 13—and Lockwood's pal—as best man. "She wanted an intimate gathering of family and friends," says wedding planner Kara Keaney. "It was unusual, personal and beautiful—just like she envisioned."

NO PEANUT-BUTTER-AND-BANANA SANDWICHES: Dinner, a nine-course feast fit for a sumo wrestler, lasted more than three hours and included fried flounder, mackerel sushi, deep-fried crab, yellowtail with foie gras, and rice dumplings with lobster and green soup. Lisa Marie "wanted traditional Japanese food," says Keaney. Guests received matching place cards featuring red and gold ribbons decorated with cranes, which symbolize longevity.

ERINN BARTLETT & OLIVER HUDSON

"It was a celebration of being together and of everyone we love," says Oliver (center with, from left to right, Boston Russell, Kurt Russell, Bartlett, Goldie Hawn, Wyatt Russell and Kate Hudson).

THE GANG'S ALL HERE: The seaside nuptials at the Mexican resort One & Only Palmilla were just as much a reunion for Hudson, 30, and Bartlett, 33. On hand to celebrate was Hudson's entire extended clan: his mom, Goldie Hawn; her longtime love, Kurt Russell; their son Wyatt and Russell's son Boston; Hudson's younger sister Kate; her husband, Chris Robinson, and their son Ryder.

NOW AND ZEN: "We tried to be as untraditional as possible," says Hudson, who exchanged personally written vows with his actress wife in a 30-minute Buddhist ceremony. "The truth is, your wedding day is insane. You're standing up there, and people are talking about your love, and you don't know what's happening." Adds Bartlett: "It's so emotional and intimate, you almost forget everyone else who is there."

LIKE MIDDLE SCHOOL MINUS "STAIRWAY TO HEAVEN": In addition to a dinner of strip steak, red snapper and a three-tiered chocolate cake, the 94 guests were treated to a memorable first dance to George Harrison's version of "If Not for You." "We were kissing and staring into each other's eyes," says Bartlett. "We felt like we were at our eighth-grade prom."

TOM CRUISE & KATIE HOLMES

WHEN IN ROME, DO AS THE ROMANTICS: Tom Cruise, 44, and Katie Holmes, 28, wed quietly in a no-frills affair . . . nah, not really. TomKat, the übercouple, staged a blockbuster wedding in a 15th-century castle outside Rome Nov. 18 before more than 150 guests including Jennifer Lopez, Brooke Shields, Jim Carrey and Will Smith. Highlights and details included thousands of roses, a serenade by Andrea Bocelli, fireworks and Cruise's son Connor, 11, carrying the couple's baby daughter Suri down the aisle. "It's crazy how beautiful it is," said guest Jenna Elfman. "It's nutty in a good way."

FRISKY BUSINESS: The newlyweds' first smooch "was never-ending," said Giorgio Armani, who designed the groom's navy blue tux and the bride's Swarovski crystal-studded gown. "Some guests had to shout 'Stop!'"

I FEEL THE NEED . . . FOR KARAOKE: When a deejay cranked up "You've Lost That Lovin' Feeling," Cruise couldn't resist reprising his *Top Gun* moment. "I respect men who are not afraid to show their feelings," Holmes's dad, Martin, said in his toast. Good thing, that.

Cruise and Holmes (with Suri, right) wed at Odescalchi Castle in a ceremony "every little girl dreams of," said a guest.

"WONDERFUL...

JUST GREAT"

—JOHN, ON EXCHANGING
VOWS WITH FURNISH

ELTON JOHN & DAVID FURNISH

"SATURDAY NIGHT'S ALRIGHT" (BUT WEDNESDAY NIGHT IS EVEN BETTER): Sir Elton John and David Furnish exchanged vows on Dec. 21 at Windsor's Guildhall in a midweek civil ceremony—on the very day that England legalized same-sex partnerships. The service, which ended in a teary kiss between John, 58, and Furnish, 43, "was very moving," said Furnish's dad, Jack. "It's one of the happiest days of our lives."

DOG, ON IT: Despite Guildhall's no-pet policy, the grooms insisted that the best man—their spaniel, Arthur—gain admittance.

SHUFFLING ROOM ONLY: Guests waited in a slow-moving line for 90 minutes to enter the reception. On the 700-person list: Elizabeth Hurley, Eric McCormack, Hugh Grant and Sharon Stone. Inside the white tents (decorated with 90,000 roses), partygoers dined on roast lamb and pink-champagne truffles.

ELTON'S NIGHT OFF: Joss Stone did the musical honors, singing the Beach Boys' "God Only Knows."

The couple wed at Windsor's Guildhall (left), and fans showed their support outside: One group hung a sign that read, "Go For It Elt & David!"

AMBER FREY & ROBERT HERNANDEZ

HOWDY NEIGHBOR: Scott Peterson's former girlfriend found someone on the right side of the law in corrections officer Hernandez, 37, who proposed after a June trip to Disneyland. "Our kids get along," Hernandez, who lived a few doors away from Frey's Clovis, Calif., home, told her father. (Each has two children.) "And I really want to be married."
FAMILY FREYS: With family looking on, Frey, 31, and Hernandez tied the knot in a small outdoor ceremony overlooking Lake Tahoe's Emerald Bay.

AVRIL LAVIGNE & DERYCK WHIBLEY

MAKING BEAUTIFUL MUSIC TOGETHER: Lavigne, 21, began dating Sum 41 singer Whibley, 26, in 2004. The Canadian couple were engaged a year later.
PUNK ROCKER TURNED PRINCESS: With nary a black-painted fingernail, the onetime tomboy embraced a much softer side for her July 15 wedding. Gliding down the aisle amid, says a guest, "more roses than I've ever seen in my life," the Vera Wang-clad Lavigne looked "just exquisite."

MATT HOOVER & SUZY PRESTON

BIG LOVE: They met on the weight-loss reality show *The Biggest Loser* in 2005, and Matt popped the question on the *Today* show. For their nuptials Sept. 19 they chose a secluded beach at the Grand Lido Negril resort in Jamaica and a smaller audience: Ten family members attended.

DIET OR TRY IT? When it came to the wedding cake, they dug into a traditional Jamaican confection and sipped pineapple cider.

TIME OUT: "There are no clocks anywhere," Suzy said of another resort on the island where they enjoyed an eight-day honeymoon. "We've really adopted the 'no problem' attitude."

339 lbs.   227 lbs.

THROUGH THICK AND THIN

A wrestling coach and motivational speaker, Hoover, 30, was *Losers* big winner, dropping 157 lbs. and picking up the $250,000 prize. Preston, also 30 and a hairdresser, came in third after dropping 95 lbs. "We still get our workouts in," Matt said. "If we don't we'll be back on *Loser* after all the food they serve down here."

All hands on mom: Brooke Shields bonds with her newborn daughter, Grier (left); older sis Rowan joins in.

LITTLE STARS

From Suri and Shiloh to Gwen's baby boy, plenty of big-name bundles of joy made their world premiere in 2006

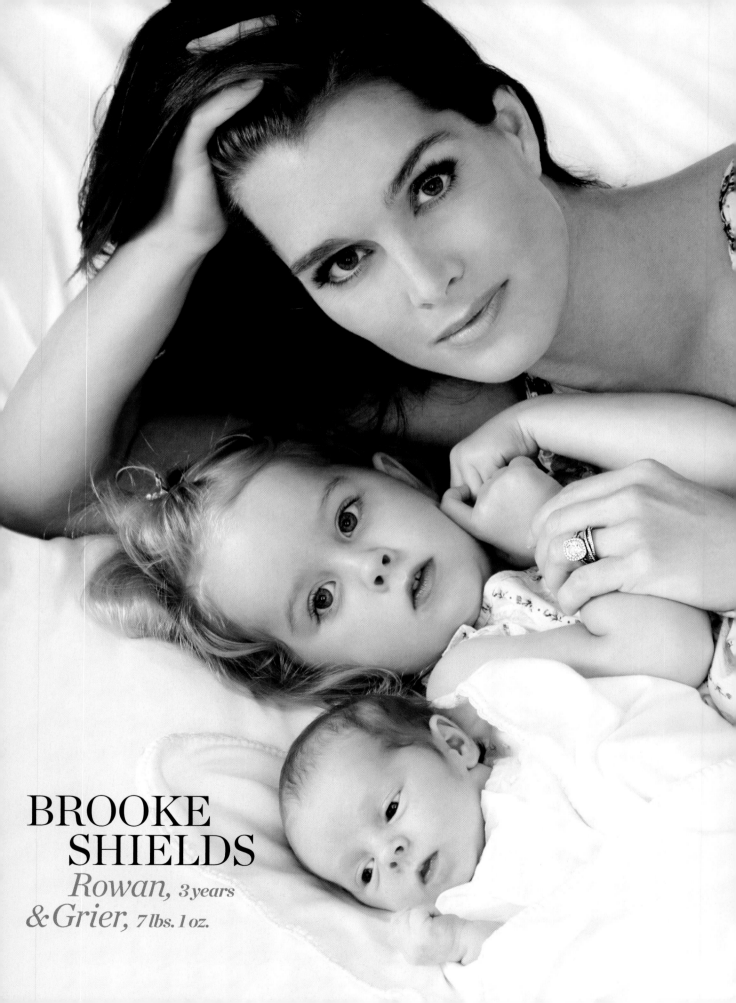

BROOKE
SHIELDS
Rowan, 3 years
& Grier, 7 lbs. 1 oz.

This pregnancy has been a lot easier," radiant second-time mom-to-be Brooke Shields, 41, said in a ringing understatement prior to the birth of daughter Grier Hammond on April 18. Almost three years before, Shields endured a 24-hour labor to deliver daughter Rowan, who was conceived with her husband, writer Chris Henchy, 42, after six failed in vitro fertilization treatments. This time around, as Shields was preparing for treatments to have another baby, her doctor informed her she was already pregnant. As Grier's due date approached, Shields's excitement was not dampened by the possibility of a recurrence of the frightening bout of postpartum depression she suffered after Rowan's birth, chronicled in her 2005 memoir *Down Came the Rain*. "If it happens, I'll recognize the symptoms and know what works," said Shields, who found relief in antidepressant medication (which she stopped taking) and therapy. "I'm going in so much stronger." And less annoyed. On this occasion, she did not have to endure criticism from Tom Cruise, who had decried her use of antidepressants to battle depression and whose own baby girl was born in the same L.A. hospital on the same day as Grier. In August, Cruise went to Shields's house and apologized; she accepted.

"I want Rowan to have a best friend out of this," Brooke, herself an only child, said before Grier's birth. "And someone else to deal with me when I'm older!"

DONALD & MELANIA TRUMP

Barron, *8 lbs. 8 oz.*

Barron, you're sired. With a name fit for his lofty lineage, the littlest emperor of the Trump dynasty made his debut March 20. The Donald's first child with wife Melania, 36, and fifth overall, Barron William ("We just liked the names," said his proud pop) is "going to be a great boy and hopefully a great man someday," predicts Trump, 60. He'll certainly have a head start. The small scion already has his own floor in Manhattan's Trump Tower complete with nursery, kitchen, living room and nanny's quarters, although he frequently sleeps in a crib next to Mom and Dad. Says hands-on mom Melania: "I like to spend every minute with him." Barron should enjoy the attention while he can. A few days after his birth, Melania noted on her Web site that she will be giving her baby "all the TLC he needs, and then I will get back to work [modeling]."

These are the golden years, obviously, for young Barron Trump. Saith The Donald: "The baby is beautiful, and Melania's a beautiful mother."

MADONNA
David Banda, 1 year old

Madonna seems to relish controversy, but even she didn't expect the public scorching that followed her planned adoption of a 1-year-old boy, David Banda, in Malawi in early October. After the arrangements became public, British and American tabloids strafed the singer—who helps fund six orphanages in that country—alleging that she had used her celebrity clout to circumvent Malawian adoption rules. Madonna, 48, calling the uproar "shocking," bluntly denied the accusation and added, "I say to those people, shame on you for discouraging other people from wanting to do the same thing." It didn't help that David's father, Yohane Banda, 32, flip-flopped when talking about the adoption, saying at one point he thought he was letting go of David only temporarily. He has since proclaimed, "I gave David to Madonna with all my heart." The toddler is now thriving with Madonna's children Lourdes, 10, and Rocco, 6. And while Madonna must wait 18 months for final approval on the adoption, she is already thinking long-term and says she is excited about giving her new son "an education and a chance for a better life." Says the new mom: "David is amazing."

It's a boy! And a girl! After nearly seven years of trying to conceive, the Oscar-nominated actress and her husband, *Law & Order: Criminal Intent* actor Courtney B. Vance, 46, welcomed twins Bronwyn

ANGELA BASSETT

Slater Josiah, 5 lbs. 2 oz.
Bronwyn Golden, 6 lbs. 2 oz.

"We continually try to go back to the way we used to do things," says Vance. "We have to say, 'Wait, there are a couple of new sheriffs in town!'"

Golden (left) and Slater Josiah via a surrogate mother on Jan. 27. "There are a whole lot of avenues to have a child," says Bassett, 48. "And we were on, like, the next-to-the-last street." The performers, who met at the Yale School of Drama, are reveling in their newest roles. "There were so many offers to go to this or that Oscar party," Bassett said. "It was a lot more fun to sit and gaze at my two little stars."

DREW LACHEY
Isabella Claire, 7 lbs. 2 oz.

Looks like the *Dancing with the Stars 2* winner and 98° singer has found a future partner to dip and twirl. Since the March 23 birth of daughter Isabella Claire, Lachey, 30, and his choreographer wife, Lea, have discovered their footing as parents, with the proud papa singing anything from Sly and the Family Stone to opera to keep her happy. "She's an angel," says uncle and godfather Nick Lachey, who set up a crib at his house in case Isabella needs a babysitter. "Thank goodness she looks like her mom."

ADAM SANDLER
Sadie Madison

The onscreen Big Daddy became one in real life May 6 when the actor and his wife of three years, Jackie, 32, welcomed their first child, Sadie Madison, in Los Angeles. "I'm looking forward to her knowing who I am," Sandler, 40, told *Good Morning America*'s Charles Gibson in June. "Right now she looks at me and stares right through me as if to say, 'Who are you? Why are you here? What do you got to do with me?'" While he's happy revising his role as the water boy (left), Sandler isn't exactly hands-on in other areas. "I see the diapers go on and cheer my wife for doing such a good job," he told the *Chicago Sun-Times*. "I'll also say, 'Honey, good feeding! Way to go! Nice milk!'"

"I'm the example of what she'll look for in a husband-to-be," says Lachey. "If I show her and her mother love, that's the best gift I can give."

NADIA COMANECI
Dylan Paul, 4 lbs. 10 oz.

With seven gold medals between Comaneci and husband Bart Conner, the married Olympic gymnasts have had many triumphant moments. But they might have saved the best one for June 3, when they welcomed first child Dylan Paul in Oklahoma City, Okla., about 20 miles from their gymnastics academy in Norman. "I've heard people talk about unconditional love," says Conner, 48, "but this is a powerful feeling." The Romanian-bred Comaneci, 45, nicknamed her tumbler Gogosel—"little donut" in her native tongue. While Conner claims that gymnastics "is not our dream for him," he can't help but notice Dylan's "little Popeye forearm." Looks like there's already a favorite for the 2024 Games.

MEG RYAN
Daisy True

Following a trip to China, the 45-year-old actress brought her newly adopted daughter Daisy True home to L.A. in mid-January. While she never wavered in her desire to give her son Jack, 14, a sibling, Ryan did have a change of heart when it came to the name of the baby—whom she applied to adopt in mid-2005—initially calling her Charlotte. "I thought she was a Charlotte," Ryan told Oprah in March. "She's just not—she's a Daisy."

"My favorite thing is to make him laugh," says Hart (in the nursery with Wilkerson, Mason and mutt Copper). "He's really ticklish, just like his dad."

MELISSA JOAN HART
Mason, 9 lbs.

Unfortunately for the *Sabrina the Teenage Witch* star, childbirth wasn't quite as easy as snapping her fingers. After labor was induced at 4 p.m. the previous day, Hart, 30, finally gave birth to Mason Walter Wilkerson at 4:20 a.m. on Jan. 11. "It felt like the baby was lodged in my hip," she said. "After three hours of pushing, he finally popped out!" The little guy arrived home to a pale-green nursery in the family's Spanish-style L.A. home, which was decorated with murals painted by Hart's stepmom, and an assortment of gifts, including a blanket knitted by pal Kellie Martin. Dad Mark Wilkerson, 29, lead singer and guitarist for the rock group Course of Nature, helped out with an original lullaby. "I love the faces Mason makes," said Hart. "I could watch him forever."

ANGELINA JOLIE
Shiloh, 7 lbs.

Well aware that their daughter would see more than her share of the spotlight in years to come, her parents made sure she entered the world far from Hollywood's glare, in the remote African nation of Namibia. Yet there was no hiding Shiloh Nouvel Jolie-Pitt's camera-ready lineage. With dad Brad's baby-blue eyes, and lips that could have come only from mom, Shiloh, born by C-section at the Cottage Medi-Clinic in the coastal town of Swakopmund May 27, earned a rave review from a key critic, big brother Maddox, 5. Brought to the clinic shortly after the birth by Jolie's brother James Haven, there to help care for him and little sister Zahara, then 1, Maddox welcomed her with open arms. "He imitated the way Brad held her just perfectly," Haven said. "Then when we got back in the car I asked, 'So what'd you think, Mad?' He just said, 'She's beautiful.'" Soon, thanks to photos published in PEOPLE June 19, the rest of the world would agree.

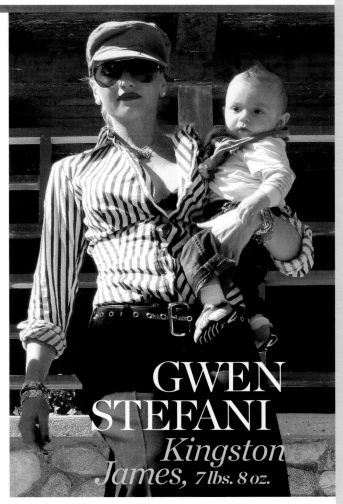

GWEN STEFANI
Kingston James, 7 lbs. 8 oz.

Rocker Gwen Stefani epitomizes edgily stylish motherhood. The L.A.M.B. clothing designer showed off her bump in kimono-style dresses and maintained her signature red pout during pregnancy. So it's no small wonder that, after the May 26 birth of Kingston James McGregor, she and husband Gavin Rossdale, 41, gave their son a fashion-forward nursery (with a glossy black crib and $300 sheets) at home in Los Feliz, Calif. Motherhood also inspired Stefani to fashion a new Harajuku Lovers line of onesies, bibs and baby T-shirts, which Stefani, 37, said are "about being super*kawaii* [Japanese for 'cute']." Also fashionable: Kingston and Mom now pencil in visits to Dad courtside as he practices tennis and make playdates with everyone from Shiloh Jolie-Pitt to Heidi Klum and Seal's kids Leni and Henry.

KATIE HOLMES
Suri, 7 lbs. 7 oz.

Talk about shop till you drop. In her final days as a mom-to-be, Holmes went on a Beverly Hills shopping blitz, snapping up some decidedly postmaternity hot pants and heels. As it happened, her days of fashion freedom were right around the corner. On April 18, Holmes, 28, and husband-to-be Tom Cruise, 44, welcomed their first child, daughter Suri (Persian for "red rose") after a complications-free birth. Things went so smoothly that Holmes left the hospital within 24 hours. The public would have to wait considerably longer to get a first peek at Suri's mop of black hair and big blue eyes. Finally the much-anticipated baby pictures—snapped by Annie Leibovitz, no less—appeared in the October issue of *Vanity Fair*, confirming one early Suri-sighter's assessment: She's "a beautiful baby."

CHARLIE
SHEEN
& DENISE
RICHARDS

BREAK

HEATHER
LOCKLEAR
& RICHIE
SAMBORA

UPS

The course of true love
never did run true—and
sometimes it just runs out.
2006 saw a Beatle and a
Bon Jovi bust-up and more

"He's been a good friend to her," says a pal of Locklear's about Spade. "They're both funny."

Heather Locklear hadn't seen this much drama since *Melrose Place*. In April, just two months after filing for divorce from her husband of 11 years, Bon Jovi guitarist Richie Sambora, the 45-year-old actress got the disturbing news that her close friend and neighbor Denise Richards, who herself was engaged in a vicious custody battle with Locklear's former *Spin City* costar Charlie Sheen, had been seeing Sambora, 47, since March. "She was shocked," a close friend says of Locklear, who ended her troubled marriage, a source tells PEOPLE, after she found provocative pictures e-mailed to Sambora by a woman they both knew. "It doesn't matter if they're separated and moving on. Either you're a friend or you're not." As recently as New Year's Eve, the gals had been tighter than ever, photographed arm-in-arm on the way to a party, with Richards even borrowing one of Locklear's outfits.

Friends of Richards, 35, insisted that her relationship with Sambora remained platonic until late March, when the pair ran into each other at the L.A. restaurant Tomodachi. "They started talking about their divorces and their kids," says a friend of Richards's. "From there it started to blossom into something more." So what about those kids? While Sambora and Locklear remained deadlocked over whether he should receive joint custody or visitation rights with daughter Ava, 9, the pair seemed to be working toward her best interests, amicably appearing together at her softball games and other functions. The same couldn't be said for Sheen and Richards, who filed a court statement in April requesting he be denied overnight visitation privileges with daughters Sam, 2, and Lola, 1, because, Richards claimed, he brought prostitutes to his home, indulged in online porn and was often on the phone with bookies making bets.

By August, the animosity eased somewhat as the two agreed to a custody agreement and to terminate Richards's restraining order. In the meantime, Richards and Sambora were growing even closer, with the actress visiting him on various stops on Bon Jovi's European summer tour. The pair even enjoyed a brief mid-tour June rendezvous in Paris—the site of Locklear and Sambora's 1994 wedding—taking in paintings at the Louvre and a romantic dinner at Montmartre's Place du Tertre.

Not that Locklear was sitting home alone the whole time. Although they both acknowledged only a "friendship," she began spending lots of time with comedian David Spade; the pair were first spotted kissing after a party for *The Showbiz Show* in March. But the surrounding chaos may have been too much to allow for anything more serious to develop: A source close to the pair acknowledged in September that they'd cooled off. "Heather is still going through a lot with Denise and Richie," the source said. "It's just too soon for her to get serious. They are still friends." As for her relationship with Richards and Sambora? "Heather's very resilient," says a friend, who notes she'll remain civil for Ava's sake. "She's a cat with nine lives. She will keep moving forward."

The newly amicable Richards and Sheen (along with his new girlfriend Brooke Mueller, 29) enjoy a local festival with the kids in October.

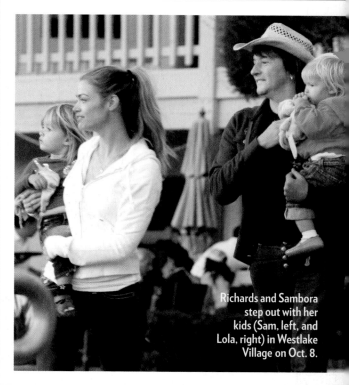

Richards and Sambora step out with her kids (Sam, left, and Lola, right) in Westlake Village on Oct. 8.

"She's a mature, hardworking girl," said Joseph Bianchi of his niece Diana (below). "She just got herself involved in a tough game."

"I have what I always wanted," Brinkley told *Redbook* in 1999. "A husband who cares about [his family] with every ounce of his being."

CHRISTIE BRINKLEY
& PETER COOK

It was the summer scandal that shocked the Hamptons. After giving a June 25 speech on global warming at a local high school, Brinkley, 52, received some news that would set her 10-year marriage afire. As the supermodel and her architect husband were leaving the auditorium, they were surprised by Southampton Village police officer Brian Platt, who confronted Brinkley with the news that Cook, 47, had been having a yearlong affair with the officer's 19-year-old stepdaughter Diana Bianchi. Two weeks after Brinkley learned about the infidelity, her publicist announced the pair had separated. Then, in mid-July, another of Cook's alleged prior affairs came to light. At that point

Brinkley bundled her two children, Jack, 11 (with third husband Ricky Taubman), and Sailor, 8, to L.A. to be with her parents. "She is totally shocked and devastated," said a friend of Brinkley's at the time. Long Island society types certainly didn't see it coming either. "This marriage has been the gold standard in the Hamptons," said R. Couri Hay, society editor for *Hamptons* magazine. Cook reached out to Brinkley via a statement to the *New York Post* that read, "I'm sorry. I'm contrite. I'm stupid. Foolish. No excuse." Despite his public apologies, his estranged wife refused to take him back, serving her soon-to-be fourth ex-husband a summons with notice (the first step toward divorce) on Sept. 13.

In February, the couple appeared to be picture perfect while attending a post-Grammy party in Beverly Hills.

BRITNEY SPEARS
& KEVIN FEDERLINE

When Britney Spears paid a surprise visit to the set of *Late Show with David Letterman* Nov. 6, she wowed host and audience alike with her buoyant smile, blonde bob wig and a bod-hugging black dress that showed off her surprisingly svelte figure, just eight weeks after giving birth to her second child. But there was more to the pop queen's return to form than Letterman or his audience knew.

After her quick cameo, Spears, 24, left the Ed Sullivan Theater in New York City and went directly to her record company's nearby offices, where she faxed her signature to her lawyers in Los Angeles. Next day, they filed divorce papers, seeking dissolution of her two-year marriage to backup dancer-turned-paramour Kevin Federline, 28, and primary custody of their two sons, Sean Preston, 1, and Jayden James.

The announcement was big news, but not—thanks to the relentless rumors, endless tabloid speculation and occasional public rows that preceded it—a big surprise.

Nonetheless, Spears's action seemed to rock Federline, who appeared despondent during a promotional tour to tout his rap CD *Playing with Fire*. "He was a sad guy," said an acquaintance who saw him in Toronto the night before the filing. Even the next day, he expressed the hope that Britney and the kids "would come and surprise me."

Spears, on the other hand, seemed upbeat. After the news became public the singer, in a low-cut dress and black fishnets, dined with friends at Manhattan's Baldoria restaurant, then trooped to a nearby Gap, bought $300 worth of sweaters and cold weather gear and went skating on the Rockefeller Center rink, happily smiling at camera-flashing fans. "She was busting out of her dress," noted a Baldoria bartender. "Maybe she's out to celebrate tonight."

APRIL 2004
The couple—and the paparazzi—hit a Santa Monica beach. "Britney's just having fun," said a source at the time, denying any hint of romance between the two.

OCTOBER 2004
A month after their surprise wedding, Britney and Kevin honeymooned in Fiji at a $1,975-a-night resort.

JUNE 2006
Britney and baby Sean strolled with Kevin.

NOVEMBER 2006
The day she filed for divorce, Spears joined four friends at the Manhattan restaurant Baldoria. Later she put on a pair of skates and took in the ice rink at Rockefeller Center.

PAUL McCARTNEY & HEATHER MILLS

Let it be? Not nearly. When the ex-Beatle and his second wife, 38, announced in May that they were ending their nearly four-year marriage, the feedback was deafening, with British tabloids slagging Mills and speculating how big a bite she'd demand of Sir Paul's $1.5 billion fortune. Now 64, he surely never thought the late-life idyll he crooned about would turn out like this–especially when, at year's end, Brit tabloids headlined allegations that the beloved pop icon had physically abused Heather. While Mills and McCartney, who filed for divorce in July, negotiate custody of daughter Beatrice, 2, one observer expects "more punches to come before the blood is on the mat."

Tabloid fever peaked in August when Mills (with cops) was locked out of Paul's London home.

LANCE ARMSTRONG
& SHERYL CROW

Within a month of meeting at a charity event in 2003, "she was all over me!" joked Lance Armstrong, 34, of fiancée Sheryl Crow. But the romance between the rocker and the rider ended in February, just before their spring wedding. Two weeks later, Crow, 44, was diagnosed with breast cancer and underwent a lumpectomy. By summer's end, she was healing on the road. One perk of her job? "There is a catharsis that I get to experience when I play," she told *Vanity Fair*.

HILARY SWANK
& CHAD LOWE

Accepting her Best Actress Oscar statuette for *Million Dollar Baby* in February 2005, Hilary Swank—who famously forgot to thank husband Chad Lowe during her 2000 win speech for *Boys Don't Cry*—made up for it, telling her husband of seven years, "You're my everything." But sentiment alone wasn't enough to fix the growing trouble in their marriage. Despite several attempts at counseling and reconciliation following their separation 11 months later, the pair finally called it quits in June, jointly deciding to divorce. "They both sincerely tried to make this work," says a friend of the pair, denying that Swank's busy acting career was a factor in the breakup. "But the simple truth is that they grew apart."

CARMEN ELECTRA & DAVE NAVARRO

Till death do us part? Not exactly. Despite the prediction of their '03 MTV reality show, the ex-Jane's Addiction rocker, 39, and former *Baywatch* babe, 34, couldn't withstand the pressures of their respective schedules. Electra initially denied rumors of a rift in March, telling PEOPLE, "We're fine! I'm not saying we have the perfect marriage . . . but we're pretty damn good. [If there were trouble], I would not walk around and pretend." When the pair—who initially posed nude on an autopsy table for their wedding invitation photos—finally announced their split July 18, it wasn't much of a separation for the couple, who met through a mutual friend in 2000. They continued living together, and at the July 23 taping of *Rock Star: Supernova*, Navarro still had his wedding ring on. Less than three weeks later, however, the marriage was officially dead, as Electra—citing irreconcilable differences—filed for divorce in L.A.

DAVID HASSELHOFF & PAMELA BACH

"I was very much in love with my wife," said the ex-*Baywatch* star, 54. "But it got to the point where it just wasn't working." The Hoff—who denied that the cause of their July split was either abuse (in court papers, Bach, 43, accused him of breaking her nose) or infidelity—had an up-and-down year. He revitalized his career as a judge on *America's Got Talent,* sliced a tendon in his arm while shaving in June and failed to board his scheduled flight after an incident at London's Heathrow Airport in July.

KATE HUDSON & CHRIS ROBINSON

In 2003 Hudson played the leading role in the romantic comedy *Le Divorce*. Now she appears headed for the real-life version. After nearly six years of marriage, the 27-year-old actress and her rocker husband, 39, decided to split in August. "I have been in an Embassy Suites in Montgomery, Ala., stuck because I want to be there for my family," she told *Vogue* a month before the split. "And there have been times when I want to scream." While the couple denied any third-party interference, Hudson's friendship with her *You, Me and Dupree* costar Owen Wilson quickly escalated after the breakup. By September, the pair were seen dining together with friends while Hudson vacationed with her and Robinson's 2-year-old son Ryder in Hawaii.

RYAN PHILLIPPE & REESE WITHERSPOON

"They seemed like the perfect Hollywood couple," said a friend. Devoted, hands-on parents to daughter Ava, 7, and son Deacon, 3, they were well known for putting family first. So it came as a shock to those close to them on Oct. 30 when Witherspoon, 30, and Phillippe, 32, announced they were separating after seven years. "We are heartbroken and worried," said Phillippe's mother. "This is devastating. We just hope things can work out." Indeed, the fact that the couple had often talked publicly about the work both of them put into the marriage made the end even more dispiriting. Said one friend: "This is so sad."

EDDIE MURPHY & NICOLE MURPHY

Their April divorce, with the couple agreeing on joint custody of their five children, seemed amicable. But fans had to wonder when Nicole uttered a diss that even the *Dr. Dolittle* set could understand: "Eddie can be a fuddy-duddy," his wife of 12 years told *Essence*. As if to prove her wrong, Murphy, 45, soon began globe-trotting with none other than Scary Spice (a.k.a. Melanie Brown of the Spice Girls). As for Nicole, 38, "I'm going to be just fine," she said.

MIKE MYERS & ROBIN RUZAN

Now they're split peas. Referred to as "two peas in a pod" by pal Alanis Morissette in 2004, the *Austin Powers* star and his wife surprised many friends when they ended their 12-year marriage in December 2005. Long admired for having one of Hollywood's most durable relationships, neither Myers, 43, nor Ruzan, 42, an actress and comedy writer he often called his muse, would say why they lost their mojo.

ANDY MILL
& CHRIS EVERT

For 18 years it looked like a love match. Then in October, tennis great Chris Evert, 52, and her husband, former Olympic skier Andy Mill, 53, announced they were getting divorced. Though the couple seemed outwardly happy and devoted to their three sons, ages 10 to 15, friends note that Mill, now a champion fly fisherman, and Evert, who share homes in Florida and Aspen, spent a great deal of time apart. Said a source: "He was always fishing, and she was doing her tennis camps." Even so, the split took close friends by surprise. "This is a bombshell," said tennis commentator Bud Collins, a longtime pal who recently visited the couple. "They seemed so happy, they had a new home. I don't think anyone would have ever suspected this."

PRINCE
& MANUELA
NELSON

She's now the Woman Formerly Known as Prince's Second Wife. During the course of their 4 ½-year marriage, the purple pair—who wed in Hawaii on New Year's Eve 2001—maintained a low profile, occasionally appearing together at awards shows and Lakers games. The reclusive pop star, 48, who was married to dancer Mayte Garcia from 1996 to 2000, first met the Toronto native when she began working at his charitable foundation. Prince will no doubt continue being Prince: He was sued by NBA player Carlos Boozer in January for painting his trademark symbol, purple stripes and the number 3121, on the exterior of the West Hollywood house the hoopster was renting him. (The suit was dismissed.) Manuela, 30, who filed for divorce in May, has put her energy into the release of her own home fragrance line.

1 MATT LeBLANC
& MELISSA McKNIGHT

So much for a Happy New Year. Barely two weeks into 2006, the *Friends* actor, 39, told his wife of three years that he was moving out of their Encino, Calif., home. Worse, he'd been seeing another woman, *Joey* costar Andrea Anders, 31. "It was very sudden," said McKnight friend Kelly Phillips. "She was absolutely blindsided." The couple have a daughter, Marina, 2, and McKnight has two kids from an earlier marriage. Adds a LeBlanc acquaintance: "Matt was finally realizing that maybe he just wasn't meant to be married. And that's a bad thing when you have a family counting on you to be there for them."

SHANNA MOAKLER & TRAVIS BARKER

"I cried a lot. I thought this was the man I'd grow old with," *Dancing with the Stars* contestant Moakler, 31, told PEOPLE after Barker, also 31, filed for divorce in August and told the press she'd cheated on him and neglected their kids. ("My No. 1 priority is my children," he said. "Shanna didn't have that same feeling.") Moakler, Miss USA 1995, denied she had strayed. "I was 100 percent faithful to that man," she said, adding that Barker, the former Blink-182 drummer and her costar on MTV's *Meet the Barkers* reality show, had worn her down with his suspicions. "When he left," she said, "I was almost relieved. I wasn't tiptoeing around the house afraid to say anything." And those rumors that were floating around about her ex and Paris Hilton? "I'm closing the door and moving forward," she told PEOPLE. "I'm a mom. I've got three kids. I'm a role model."

CHARLES SPENCER & CAROLINE

They met as students at Oxford, went on to wed others and got together after their marriages broke up. In 2001, the earl and the former nursery school teacher tied the knot at Althorp, the family seat where Spencer's sister Princess Diana is buried. Spencer, 42 , once said, "I've found someone I respect and adore and I feel very happy." But in early September, five years and two children later, he and Caroline, 39, broke up.

WHITNEY HOUSTON
& BOBBY BROWN

1

She was raised on gospel music. He was a pop soul fan from the streets of Boston's Roxbury section. And their 14-year marriage seemed at times like an out-of-control roller-coaster ride, with a 1997 separation, rumors of drug use and infidelity and, to cap it off, *Being Bobby Brown,* the 2005 reality show that redefined the concept of Too Much Information. In May, Brown told PEOPLE, "We are happily married." In October, Houston filed for divorce.

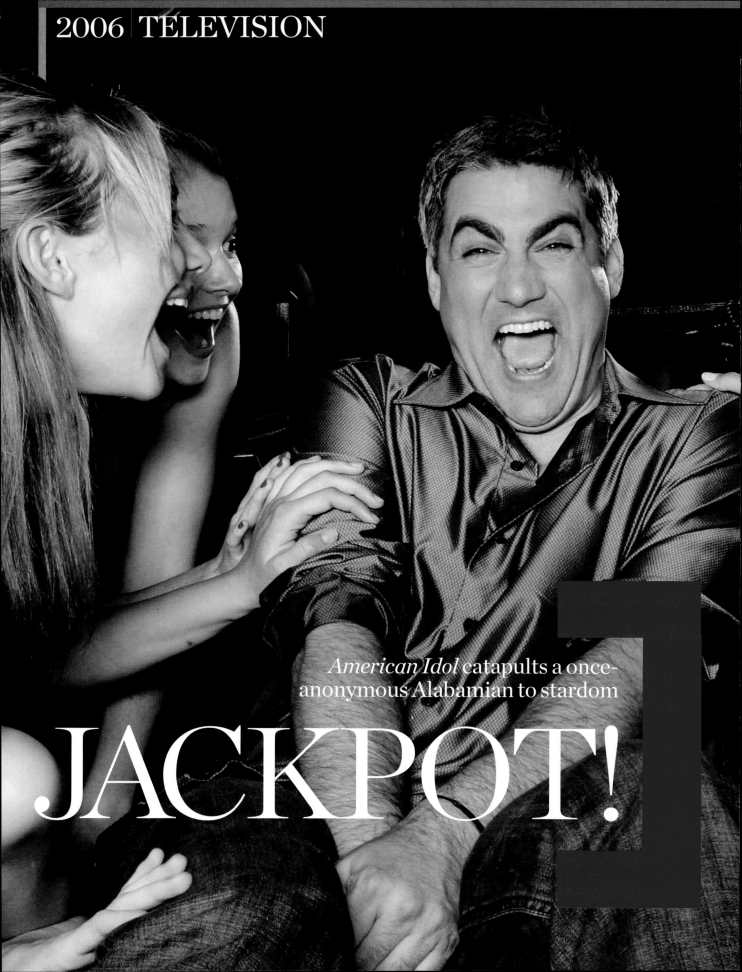

American Idol catapults a once-
anonymous Alabamian to stardom

JACKPOT!

1

"Wooooooo!" is the cry of his Soul Patrol fans. "I'm single," says Hicks (posing in a limo). "This is nice to hear."

TAYLOR HICKS

The whirlwind rise from Alabama bar crooner to *Idol* star began in a hurricane. Making his escape from New Orleans as Katrina hit last year, Hicks was offered a seat on a plane going anywhere he wanted. "So I went to Las Vegas," recalls the 29-year-old, who, upon finding that *American Idol* try-outs were in progress there, went all in. "I auditioned and here I am." Crowned the fifth-edition *Idol* after beating out Katharine McPhee before 43 million Idolators on May 24, Hicks scored appearances on *Tonight* and *Ellen,* top billing on the American Idols Live! tour and—best of all for a journeyman rocker who spent 10 years on the Birmingham bar circuit, fruitlessly cold-calling radio deejays to get them to spin his demo CDs—a $1 million recording contract for a debut album overseen by industry legend Clive Davis. For Hicks, who won over the TV audience with high-energy performances, the formula is nothing new. "At first he was a curiosity, with all his dancing and twitching around," says a booker from the Flora-Bama Lounge on the Florida-Alabama line where he got his start, "but then everyone realized this guy could really sing."

STAR JONES REYNOLDS & BARBARA WALTERS

Dedicated *View*ers enjoy the often-feisty give-and-take between host Barbara Walters and her chatty gal pals on ABC's morning coffee klatch. But when Star Jones Reynolds took her boss's hand during the live show June 27 and announced, "I will not be returning as cohost next year," Walters, *The View*'s creator, was stunned. "I felt, this morning, betrayed," Walters later told PEOPLE, explaining that Reynolds had been offered a face-saving send-off when informed months earlier that her contract would not be renewed. Star acknowledged that her knack for over-the-top self-promotion alienated fans. "But," she said of leaving, "it hurts."

Boom, Boom: Learning that her critic Rosie O'Donnell was joining the show she was leaving was a one-two punch, Star said.

UGLY BETTY

The Devil Wears *huaraches*? ABC's surprise hit stars America Ferrera as the bushy-browed nonfashionista at *Mode*, a *Vogue*-like mag where she fends off taunts from coworkers. Produced by Salma Hayek, *UB* is a remake of the Colombian telenovela *Yo Soy Betty, la Fea* ("I Am Betty, the Ugly One"). It became hot, says a TV insider, because "women love shows about ugly ducklings who make it."

PROJECT RUNWAY

Few shows featured more behind-the-seams drama than Bravo's cable sensation. Tears flowed, fur flew, Vincent went pantless in the workroom, and, finally, *Runway*'s judges named Jeffrey Sebelia (below) the winner. Says *Runway*'s Tim Gunn: "He's adept at taking what's happening on the street and making it into fashion with a capital *F*."

McDREAMY VS. McSTEAMY

Those cheatin' hearthrobs Drs. McDreamy and McSteamy compete for Dr. Meredith *Grey's Anatomy*. How they match up:

DREAMY	STEAMY
REAL STATS	
Patrick Dempsey, 40, a former juggler	Eric Dane, 33, an ex-construction worker
SO McNAMED	
Because he "is so adorable," said show creator Shonda Rhimes	For lust fog formed during his shower scenes
STAYS FIT BY	
Driving race cars and exercise	Weightlifting and anything competitive
WHO'S HOTTEST?	
"He asks me when my calender is coming out," Dane says	"I don't feel any competition with Patrick"
SECOND OPINION	
"Girls go crazy for him," says costar Ellen Pompeo	Hot enough to sleep with Dreamy's wife and turn on Dr. Grey

On the big screen, a swashbuckler flounced, a woman turned blue, and the cars would *not* shut up

PIRATES & MUTANTS & CARS, OH, MY!

PIRATES OF THE CARIBBEAN: DEAD MAN'S CHEST

It was keelhauled by some of the same critics who had raved about *Pirates of the Caribbean: The Curse of the Black Pearl,* the first installment of the swashbuckling trilogy. But with Johnny Depp reprising his star turn as campy Capt. Jack Sparrow (and Keira Knightley and Orlando Bloom returning as the sword-crossed lovers), *Dead Man's Chest* found treasure at the box office, grossing $421 million domestically. Part 3, *At World's End,* is due in 2007. Yo, ho, ho, me hearty studio accountants!

X-MEN: THE LAST STAND

Wolverine snarled, Storm did something about the weather and Rogue struggled with her intimacy issues. Oh, and Magneto rearranged the Golden Gate Bridge. Sure, they carry a lot of metaphorical baggage, but these mutants still know how to put on a good show. And with new director Brett Ratner replacing Bryan Singer, they also levitated into a $100 million opening weekend take. Must be some kind of Mystique.

CARS

Pixar went NASCAR with an anthropomorphic cast of stock-car characters, from the crusty old Hudson (voiced by Paul Newman) to the hot little Porsche (Bonnie Hunt) to the arrogant speedster in need of a lesson in humanity (Owen Wilson). On opening weekend, with gas selling for close to $3 a gallon in the real world, it pulled in more than $60 million, parallel parking itself in the No. 1 spot. V-room!

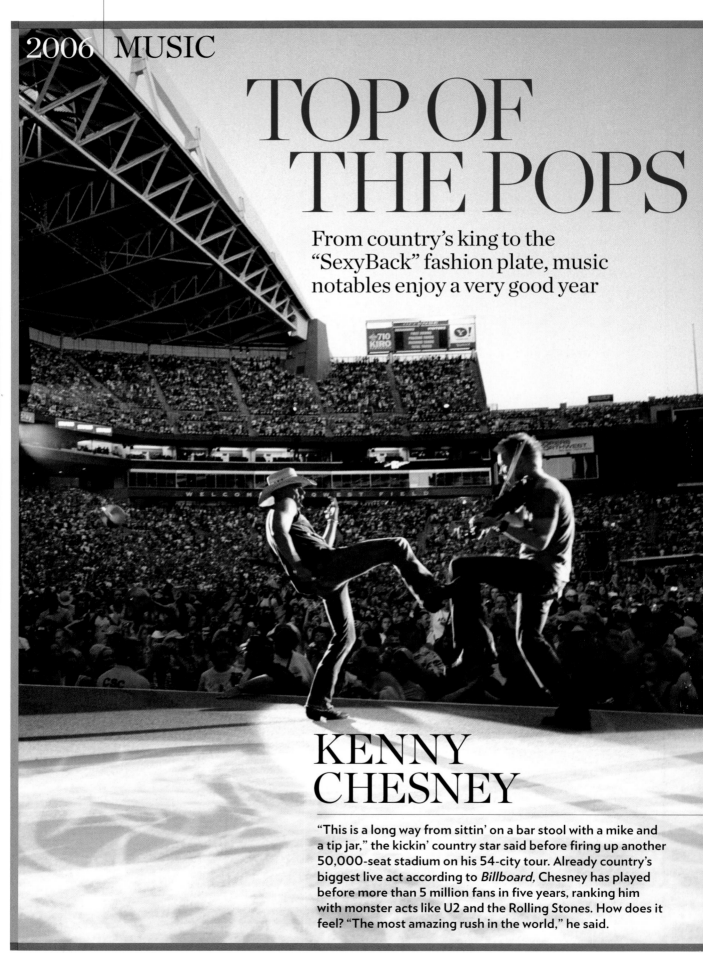

TOP OF THE POPS

From country's king to the "SexyBack" fashion plate, music notables enjoy a very good year

KENNY CHESNEY

"This is a long way from sittin' on a bar stool with a mike and a tip jar," the kickin' country star said before firing up another 50,000-seat stadium on his 54-city tour. Already country's biggest live act according to *Billboard*, Chesney has played before more than 5 million fans in five years, ranking him with monster acts like U2 and the Rolling Stones. How does it feel? "The most amazing rush in the world," he said.

BEYONCE

After celebrating her 25th birthday Sept. 4 with a new CD, *B'Day*, the multitasking Miss B readied for the release of the movie *Dreamgirls*.

DIXIE CHICKS

Their album *Taking the Long Way* debuted at No. 1 on the country charts, but their perceived Bush-bashing led to slow ticket sales—and some canceled concerts—in Dixie.

SHAKIRA

Shake, shake, shake: "Hips Don't Lie" was the fastest selling digital single ever (266,500 downloads in one week).

JUSTIN TIMBERLAKE

His second solo album, *FutureSex/LoveSounds,* is No. 1. His single "SexyBack" is all but inescapable. Now he's pulled a Diddy and launched his own fashion line with buddy Trace Ayala. But unlike others, he doesn't sew his name onto any of his William Rast denim creations. "I don't want to look like a celebrity who is cashing in on celebrity," he said.

FERGIE

Credited with invigorating the Black Eyed Peas with her platinum pipes, she left the pod (temporarily) to hit No. 1 with her swinging single "London Bridge." Critics hailed her debut solo CD *The Dutchess*.

BEST
& WORST

A vision in gold chiffon, Jessica Alba mined classic Hollywood glamour. Jennifer Aniston perfected basic black, and Nicole Kidman defined heavenly white. All in all, a vintage year for red carpet couture. (And if Sarah Jessica's mad for plaid, well, to each her own woof and warp . . .)

JESSICA ALBA
"You look like an Oscar!" Cash Warren told girlfriend Alba, in Atelier Versace, between kisses on Awards night in March.

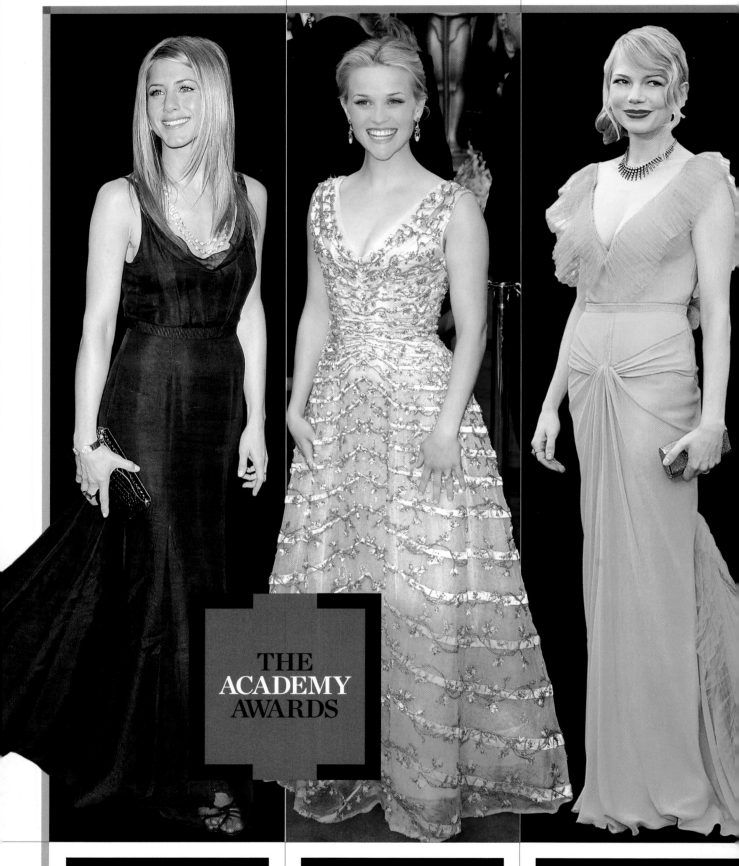

THE
**ACADEMY
AWARDS**

JENNIFER ANISTON
Rochas

REESE WITHERSPOON
Vintage Dior

MICHELLE WILLIAMS
Vera Wang

NICOLE KIDMAN
Balenciaga

UMA THURMAN
Atelier Versace

KEIRA KNIGHTLEY
Vera Wang

THE
GOLDEN
GLOBE
AWARDS

FELICITY HUFFMAN
Marchesa

TERI HATCHER
Atelier Versace

NATALIE PORTMAN
Vintage Chanel

KATE BECKINSALE
Dior by John Galliano

CHARLIZE THERON
Dior Haute Couture
by John Galliano

ZIYI ZHANG
Giorgio Armani Privé

THE
EMMY
AWARDS

EVANGELINE LILLY
Versace

CALISTA FLOCKHART
Derek Lam

HEIDI KLUM
Michael Kors

KATHERINE HEIGL
Escada

ELLEN POMPEO
Dior by John Galliano

DEBRA MESSING
Alberta Ferretti

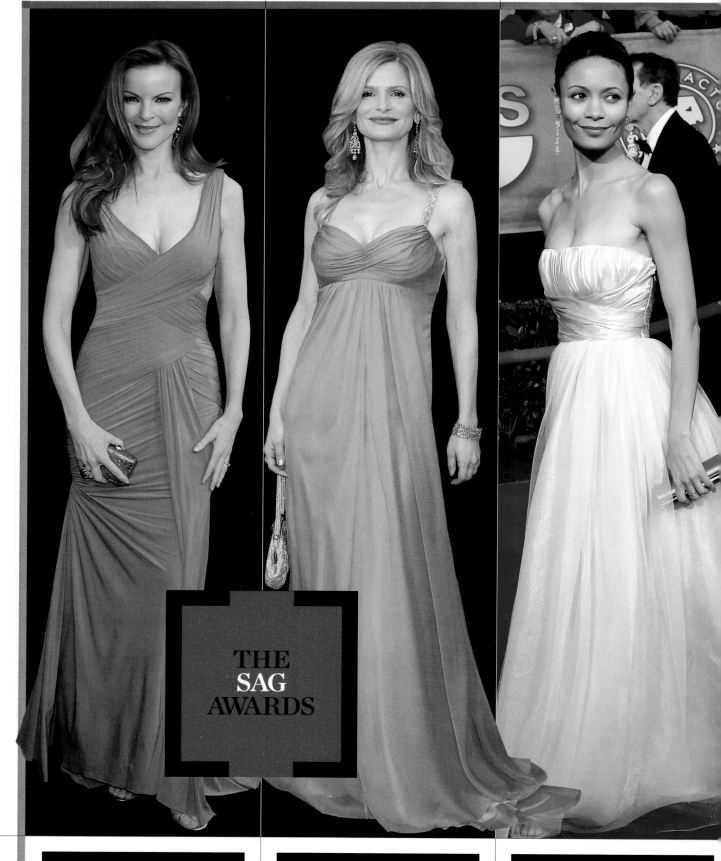

THE
SAG
AWARDS

MARCIA CROSS
Vera Wang

KYRA SEDGWICK
J. Mendel

THANDIE NEWTON
Luisa Beccaria

SANDRA BULLOCK
Angel Sanchez

MARISKA HARGITAY
Carolina Herrera

EVA LONGORIA
Badgley Mischka

THE
CFDA
AWARDS

RIHANNA
Max Azria Atelier

AMERIE
BCBG Max Azria

ALICIA KEYS
Vera Wang

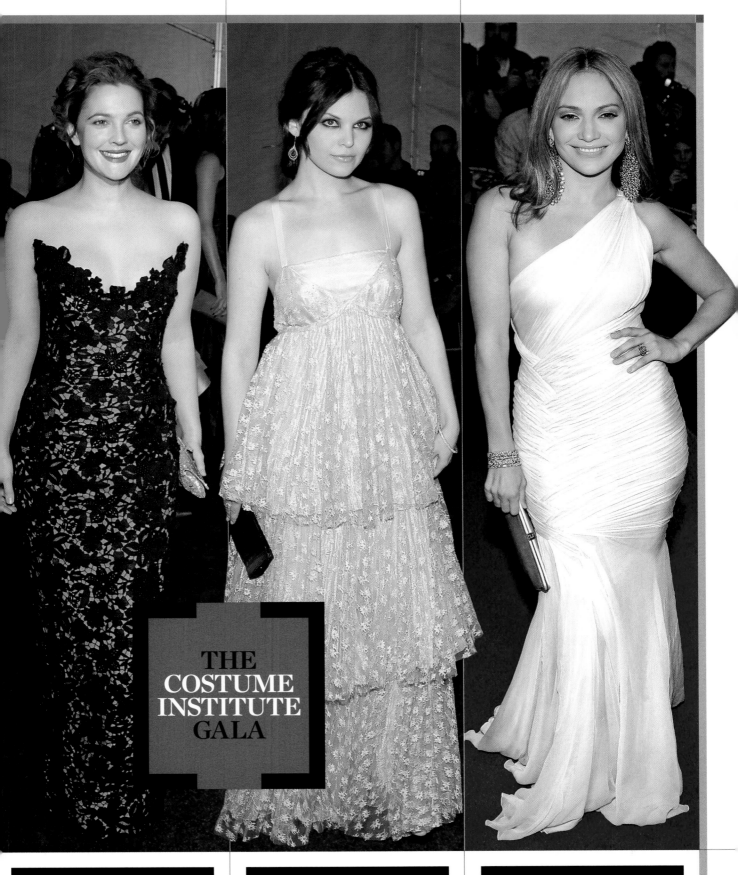

THE COSTUME INSTITUTE GALA

DREW BARRYMORE
Oscar de la Renta

GINNIFER GOODWIN
Marc Jacobs

JENNIFER LOPEZ
Versace

JAY-Z
CONCERT
AFTER-
PARTY

MTV VIDEO
MUSIC
AWARDS

CANNES
FILM
FESTIVAL

THE OUT & ABOUT AWARDS

BEYONCE
Roberto Cavalli

HALLE BERRY
Vicky Tiel

NICOLE RICHIE
Ralph Lauren

MTV VIDEO
MUSIC
AWARDS

*YOU, ME
AND
DUPREE* PREMIERE

*THE DEVIL
WEARS
PRADA* PREMIERE

CHRISTINA AGUILERA
Versace

KATE HUDSON
Diane von Furstenberg

ANNE HATHAWAY
Prada

COSTUME
INSTITUTE
GALA

ELTON
JOHN
OSCAR
PARTY

BET
APPEARANCE

**MAYBE
NOT
SO *HAUTE***

EVA MENDES
She's had it up to ear.

PARIS HILTON
Plumed heirhead. Extremely
rare east of Hollywood.

BEYONCE
Wilma Flintstone's big night out?

COSTUME
INSTITUTE
GALA

THE
OSCARS

BET
AWARDS

SARAH JESSICA PARKER
Aye, that's a bonny blanket!

LAUREN HUTTON
Madam, your wampum is showing.

KELIS
The aura of . . . origami?

THAT'S *SO* 2006

Taking a cue from '80s styles, stars update looks that were hot when they were toddlers

GLOVELETS

How does a star show she's still "street"? By donning the oh-so-tough glovelet . . . by Chanel, of course.

MINIS

Let the gams begin! Celebs took the (thigh) high road, choosing hemlines that skirted sartorial convention.

LEGGINGS

Leggings added an '80s vibe— and rock and roll edge—to summer dressing. (Question: Are acid-washed jeans next?)

SCARVES + SUNGLASSES

How to guess your age? By whether you respond, "That looks like A) Jackie O; B) Ali MacGraw; or C) Axl Rose!"

WAIST BELTS

Accessorizing was a cinch with wide belts positioned higher and tighter than last year's low-slung versions.

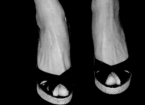

SKINNY JEANS

Celebs booted the boot cut in favor of tight, drainpipe jeans—footwear- and blouse-choice chaos ensued.

BLACK NAIL POLISH

Because the trend's acolytes (Jessica Simpson, Jennifer Lopez, Eva Mendes) just scream "goth," no?

[1961-2006]

DANA REEVE

After her Superman stumbled, she took care of him—and then faced her own illness with courage and grace

"To be honest," said Dana (below, with Chris in 1999 and opposite page, with Chris and Will near their home in 2002), "I don't have any more down days than anybody else."

Reeve (in 1998) never gave up her singing career.

No one could have blamed Dana Reeve if, sometime in the year or so before her death on March 6 at age 44, she came to the conclusion that life was a cruel and unfair undertaking and turned her face away from it. After all, 17 months earlier she had lost her husband, *Superman* actor Christopher Reeve, 52, whom she had taken care of for nearly 10 years after he was paralyzed in a horseback-riding accident. Four months later, her mother, Helen Morosini, 71, died of ovarian cancer. And on the night of Thanksgiving 2005, her father, Charles, 72, suffered a stroke at her home in Pound Ridge, N.Y. Yet Reeve, diagnosed with Stage 4 lung cancer in July 2005, carried on gamely and graciously. "Her cancer didn't scare her away from living her life," says cancer survivor Lance Armstrong, who was introduced to Dana by mutual friend Robin Williams.

Reeve continued her public efforts as an advocate for embryonic-stem-cell research and immersed herself in the work of the Christopher Reeve Foundation, which is dedicated to healing spinal cord injuries. At the same time, she dedicated herself to preparing a safe and secure future for the couple's only child, Will, then 13, an eighth-grader. "They were very tight," Dana's older sister Dr. Deborah Huschle told PEOPLE. "They had to stick together from a very early point. A lot of her life was being a hockey mom." To keep Will among the people he grew up with, Dana arranged for him to live with the family of one of his closest friends in New York's Westchester County.

An actress and singer who grew up in Edgemont, N.Y., Dana met her husband when she was performing in a cabaret in Williamstown, Mass., and he was there. They were married just three years when he broke his neck while competing in an equestrian competition in Culpeper, Va. Paralyzed from the neck down, he spent the rest of his life in a wheelchair on life support. "One of Chris's biggest messages to other disabled people was, 'Be in other people's faces. You're as good as anyone else,'" said Dana's friend Michael Manganiello. "Dana was the same way with the cancer. It was like, 'I'm not going to hide.'"

Dana battled her disease aggressively, cheerfully keeping her friends apprised of her progress. "I've lost some weight," one of her e-mails read, "but I can wear the jeans I used to wear in college, and I actually look pretty good in them."

On Jan. 12 Reeve sang Carole King's "Now and Forever" at a Madison Square Garden ceremony honoring New York Rangers star Mark Messier. It would be her last public appearance. One day near the end, family and friends gathered at her bedside. "She was still getting radiation," says her sister Adrienne Morosini-Heilman, "so her throat hurt. I just thought, through this whole thing, she can barely swallow and yet she kept her sense of humor. She was just a fighter."

In April 2005 Dana visited Washington, D.C., to lobby for passage of the Christopher Reeve Paralysis Act.

Following her husband's death, Reeve and son Will (at a gala in N.Y.C.) attended fund-raisers to help cure spinal injuries.

[1927-2006]

CORETTA SCOTT KING

AFTER HIS DEATH, AS IN HIS LIFE, SHE WAS MARTIN LUTHER KING JR.'S TIRELESS HELPMATE

For 15 years—until his assassination in Memphis in 1968—she was Rev. Martin Luther King Jr.'s wife and the mother of his four young children, standing by his side as the young preacher she married in 1953 became the unswerving moral voice of his generation. Then, for almost four decades, while raising her family alone, she was the keeper of the flame, proselytizing for her late husband's vision of racial justice and nonviolent social change. Coretta Scott King, who died Jan. 31 at age 78, was, said Andrew Young, the former U.S. ambassador to the United Nations, "a woman born to struggle, and she has struggled and she has overcome."

[1965-2006]

CHRIS PENN

THE *RESERVOIR DOGS* ACTOR LIVED A LIFE SHADED BY TRAGEDY AND TROUBLES

"I'm my own artist," Chris Penn once said. "Always have been and always will be." It must have been a tall order for Penn, who died on Jan. 24 at age 40. His family was steeped in showbiz. Dad Leo, who died in 1998, was a director. Then there was mother Eileen, 79, an actress, and brother Michael, 48, a composer. And towering over all of them was his brother Sean, in whose imposing artistic shadow Chris spent his working life. Chris, however, carved out a career for himself, starting with 1984's *Footloose*. His most memorable role: as the mercurial thug Eddie in 1992's cult favorite *Reservoir Dogs*. Penn, who had ballooned to over 300 lbs. at the time of his death, battled an addiction to both drugs and alcohol, brought on, he said in an interview, by the death of his 2-day-old daughter in the late 1980s. He credited Sean with helping him deal with his abuse problems.

JOHN SPENCER [1946-2005]

HIS FAMILIAR FACE GRACED TELEVISION SERIES FROM *THE PATTY DUKE SHOW* TO *THE WEST WING*

He was never the hero—but he was the straight-talking, streetwise sidekick the hero could turn to when things got rough. John Spencer, who died Dec. 16, 2005, four days before his 59th birthday, watched Harrison Ford's back in 1990's *Presumed Innocent* and handled Martin Sheen's dirty work as Chief of Staff Leo McGarry on *The West Wing*. The only son of a dump-truck driver and a waitress, the New Jersey-raised Spencer left home when he was 16 and soon landed a role on *The Patty Duke Show*. He worked steadily in theater and TV but gradually fell victim to alcoholism. Sober at the end, Spencer, his girlfriend, Patti Mariano, told PEOPLE, "was one of the good guys."

EARL WOODS [1932-2006]

HIS ABILITY TO RECOGNIZE TALENT AT AN EARLY AGE LED TO SON TIGER'S BRILLIANT CAREER

Earl Woods's "Eureka!" moment came when his son Tiger hopped out of his high chair and perfectly copied Earl's golf swing. Realizing that he had something special, Woods, who died May 3 of prostate cancer at age 74, devoted his life to helping Tiger realize his prodigious talent. It paid off: Now the only question is whether—or when—Tiger Woods will surpass Jack Nicklaus's record number of championship titles. What's remarkable is that Earl, an ex-Green Beret with two tours of duty in Vietnam, molded Tiger into a superstar without going the demanding parent-of-the-prodigy route. "He was never overbearing, never pushy," said Rudy Duran, Tiger's first golf coach. "He was just there for Tiger on every hole, supporting him." Earl lived to see Tiger win 10 majors. "The Tiger we see today," said Butch Harmon, Tiger's first pro coach, "is a product of Earl Woods."

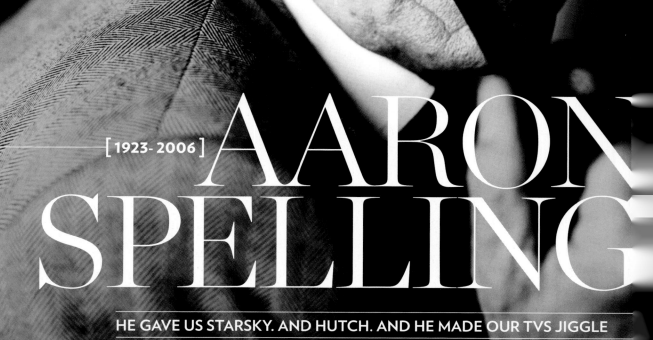

[1923-2006] AARON
SPELLING

HE GAVE US STARSKY. AND HUTCH. AND HE MADE OUR TVS JIGGLE

Starting in 1959 with his first series, *Johnny Ringo*, Spelling, who died June 23 at age 83, was destined to become a one-man TV factory. *Starsky and Hutch. The Love Boat. Fantasy Island. The Mod Squad. Hart to Hart. Charlie's Angels. Dynasty. The Colbys. T.J. Hooker. Beverly Hills, 90210. Charmed.* All his. In the 1970s and early '80s, he produced so much of ABC's prime-time programming—nearly a third—that the network was jokingly referred to as "Aaron's Broadcasting Company." Naturally, the man who gave us jiggle TV couldn't catch a break from the critics. "Unfortunately," he once said, "we often have to make the choice between 150 critics and 150 million Americans out there, and I have always felt that my job was to please [the viewers]. To entertain them." He did. *Dynasty*, for example, reached 40 million viewers at its peak, and Spelling became one of Hollywood's wealthiest men. While he was justly proud of his few critical successes— among them the AIDS drama *And the Band Played On* and *The Best Little Girl in the World*, a 1981 drama about anorexia— Spelling, the Dallas-born son of an immigrant tailor, saw very clearly where his mission lay. "I think there is a need to escape," he said. "I think it is a release valve that keeps people from blowing their brains out or having nervous breakdowns."

[1953-2006]

JUNE POINTER

THE YOUNGEST POINTER SISTER, SHE SUPPLIED THE SULTRY LEAD VOICE ON "JUMP (FOR MY LOVE)" AND "HE'S SO SHY"

Her life story sounds like the saddest of blues ballads, yet you'd never know it from listening to her sing. During the Pointer Sisters' golden years in the '70s and '80s, that was June's voice singing lead on such hits as "Jump (For My Love)." The youngest of the sisters, June, who died of cancer on April 11 at age 52, grew up in a home where singing secular songs earned a whipping from their religious parents. Yet whenever they had the house to themselves, she said in a 1981 interview, the kids would "get in the back room and beat pie pans with spoons, making that rhythm and jamming together." Her attempts at a solo career—the '83 album "Baby Sister" and an '89 self-titled solo album—didn't match her success with her sisters. The drugs that she told PEOPLE in 2000 had been a part of her life since she was 13 finally got her kicked out of the group in 1999; she returned in 2002 and left again in 2004. When she died in Santa Monica, sisters Ruth and Anita were at her side. "Ruthie took June in her arms and held her like a baby," Anita, 58, said, "until she took her last breath."

LOU [1933-2006] RAWLS

HE HAD A VOICE AS SMOOTH AS SILK, SAID SINATRA, AND RAISED MILLIONS FOR THE UNITED NEGRO COLLEGE FUND

He had what Frank Sinatra once called "the silkiest chops in the singing game." Aretha Franklin once said, "A lot of singers sound like other singers. Lou Rawls didn't sound like anyone but Lou Rawls." But the Grammy winner, who died of lung cancer Jan. 6 at age 72, was most proud of his work with *The Lou Rawls Parade of Stars* telethon, which he launched in 1979 and which has raised more than $200 million for the United Negro College Fund. Rawls, who grew up in Chicago (where he was a high school classmate of soul legend Sam Cooke), started singing in his church choir at 7. Moving on from his gospel roots, he carved out a niche as a blues and jazz singer in the '60s, then seduced a whole new generation with his '76 R&B-disco hit "You'll Never Find Another Love Like Mine." A week before he died, old friend Della Reese visited him. "We prayed together," she said. "We laughed about things from our past. And when I left, I knew that whatever happened, Lou was all right." He had, said his third wife, Nina, 36—with whom Rawls adopted son Aiden, now a 1-year-old—"an amazing heart."

BETTY [1921-2006] FRIEDAN

THE FIERY FEMINIST URGED WOMEN TO GET OUT OF THE HOUSE AND INTO THE WORLD

"Is this all?" That, in Betty Friedan's view, was the question that bedeviled the middle-class mid-20th-century American housewife, trapped, as Friedan saw it, in stultifying suburban domesticity and cut off from the life of the real world, the domain of the menfolk. *The Feminine Mystique,* her 1963 bestseller and one of the most influential books of the century, was the cri de coeur that crystallized that discontent and helped launch the women's movement. "Some people think I'm saying, 'Women of the world unite—you have nothing to lose but your men,'" she told LIFE magazine in 1963. "It's not true. You have nothing to lose but your vacuum cleaners." In 1966 Friedan, who died on Feb. 4 at age 85, helped found the National Organization for Women (she was its first president) and went on to become its most public face. Her views were soon outflanked by her more radical sisters, but her legacy lives on in the form of more equal job opportunities, maternity leave and legal abortion. "Anytime you walked down the street with Betty," says NOW cofounder Muriel Fox, "women would walk up to her and say, 'You changed my life!'"

BRUNO KIRBY

SPECIALIZING IN NEEDY, ANNOYING SIDEKICKS, HE TURNED HIS SUPPORTING ROLES INTO A FINE WHINE

Remember him as Billy Crystal's tenderfoot wingman (below) in *City Slickers*? Or as Crystal's best friend in *When Harry Met Sally*? Or in the part, which jump-started his career, as the Sinatra-obsessed limo driver in *This Is Spinal Tap*? Kirby, who died of leukemia at 57 on Aug. 14, specialized, in the words of Britain's newspaper *The Guardian*, in "fast-talking, insecure characters, always welcome onscreen but none of whom one would want to know in real life." In his own real life, though, wrote Joel Achenbach in *The Washington Post*, Kirby was "a great talent and a sweet guy—no act."

JACK WARDEN

[1920-2006]

NOT JUST ANOTHER HOLLYWOOD JAWLINE, HE PLAYED REAL PEOPLE WITH REAL JOBS

For six decades, starting with *Man with My Face* in 1951 and ending with 2000's *The Replacements*, Warden, who died July 19 at age 85, specialized in avuncular cops, crusty newspaper editors and gruff football coaches. He played father, uncle and grandfather—but never the romantic lead. Nominated twice for Oscars (for *Shampoo* and *Heaven Can Wait*) and an Emmy winner (for 1971's *Brian's Song*), the World War II vet—he fought in the Battle of the Bulge—was an everyman who brought character to the art of character acting.

[1920- 2006]

SHELLEY WINTERS

MOVIE BLONDES DIDN'T COME ANY BIGGER OR BRASSIER—OR LIVE LIFE SO LARGE

She recalled her early career thusly: "Strangled by Ronald Colman, drowned by Montgomery Clift, stabbed and drowned by Robert Mitchum, shot by Jack Palance and Rod Steiger . . . overdosed with heroin by Ricardo Montalban." But Winters, who died Jan. 14 at 85, quickly tired of playing doomed bombshells and reinvented herself as a brash character actor. She won two Best Supporting Actress Oscars—for *The Diary of Anne Frank* and *A Patch of Blue*. Her most memorable performance, however, was as the overweight former swimming champion in *The Poseidon Adventure*. In 1980 she threw a party and invited all the leading men she had slept with. The invitees, most of whom stayed away, included Brando and Lancaster. As Shelley put it, "I've had it all."

WENDY [1950-2006] WASSERSTEIN

THE PLAYFUL PLAYWRIGHT GAVE VOICE TO A GENERATION OF WOMEN WHO WERE SICK OF BEING UPSTAGED IN THE THEATER—AND IN LIFE

The Broadway plays Wendy Wasserstein attended as a young woman never showed anyone like herself onstage. "I remember going to them and thinking, 'I really like this, but where are the girls?' " she said later. So Wasserstein, who died at 55 on Jan. 30 of lymphoma, set out to populate the stage with women just like herself— smart, funny, ambivalent about love and success. "She was known for being a popular, funny playwright, but she was also a woman and a writer of deep conviction and political activism," André Bishop, artistic director of Lincoln Center Theater, told *The New York Times* right after she died. "In Wendy's plays, women saw themselves portrayed in a way they hadn't been onstage before—wittily, intelligently and seriously at the same time." Wasserstein's big breakout work was 1977's *Uncommon Women and Others,* in which "she was this amazingly original, contemporary voice for so many women," recalled the show's Swoosie Kurtz. But she is probably best remembered for *The Heidi Chronicles,* which opened on Broadway in 1989 with Joan Allen in the title role, ran for 622 performances and won Wasserstein both a Tony and a Pulitzer Prize. The night after she died, they dimmed the lights on Broadway in her honor.

BUCK OWENS [1929-2006]

HE WAS *HEE HAW*'S GENIAL HOST—AND ONE OF COUNTRY MUSIC'S GREAT HIT KICKERS

Hee Haw? The country music-and-cornpone comedy show that he cohosted with Roy Clark from 1969 to 1986 wasn't the half of it. Owens, who died March 25 at age 76, was a one-man music empire. Blending rock-and-roll rhythms with country harmonies to create the Bakersfield sound (after his neck of the woods in California), he had 20 No. 1 hits—including "Act Naturally" (later recorded by the Beatles) and "Waitin' in Your Welfare Line"—between 1959 and 1974. He also wrote Ray Charles's "Cryin' Time." Disdaining the overproduced music of Nashville, Owens was strictly roadhouse. "If it's country," he said, "I want it honky-tonk."

DENNIS [1924-2006] WEAVER

HE WAS AS UPSTANDING A COWBOY AS EVER RODE THE WEST—OR THE WEST SIDE

He didn't take only roles that required a cowboy hat—that's just how most of us remember him. Weaver, who died Feb. 24 at 81, played Chester, Marshall Dillon's sidekick on *Gunsmoke,* from 1955 to 1964. In the 1970s he was McCloud, a New Mexico lawman who wound up fighting crime in New York City. Weaver, though, had other sides. His performance as Stanley Kowalski in a 1950's Los Angeles production of *A Streetcar Named Desire* was compared favorably to Brando's on Broadway. Orson Welles cast him in 1958's *Touch of Evil.* Offscreen, Weaver devoted much of his energy to the environment, even living in a solar-powered Colorado house made from recycled tires and tin cans. "You could count on him," says Valerie Harper, who twice played his TV wife. "[He had] a wonderful American quality."

BILLY [1946-2006] PRESTON

HIS KEYBOARD TALENTS IMPRESSED THE BEATLES, THE STONES AND LITTLE RICHARD

The lineup on the title track of Billy Preston's 1969 album *That's the Way God Planned It*: George Harrison, Eric Clapton, Keith Richards, Ginger Baker. That's how much musicians revered Preston, who suffered from kidney failure and died on June 6 at age 59. A candidate to be the fifth Beatle (John Lennon asked him to join the group; that's his piano on "Get Back"), Preston also played with Little Richard (at age 15) and the Rolling Stones and cowrote Joe Cocker's anthemic "You Are So Beautiful."

[1941-2006] SLOBODAN MILOSEVIC

HIS REIGN OF TERROR LEFT MORE THAN A QUARTER OF A MILLION CIVILIANS DEAD AND A NATION TORN ASUNDER

Few leaders have left such a legacy of brutal futility: three failed wars; 250,000 civilians murdered; an entire nation sundered into its many parts. That, however, is how Serbia's ex-president Slobodan Milosevic, who died in a jail cell in The Hague on March 11 at age 64, is likely to be remembered by history. Trading Communism for virulent nationalism, he oversaw the worst European warfare since World War II. "He exploited nationalistic feelings," said Richard Dicker of Human Rights Watch. "The result was murder and mayhem." And ignominy.

MICKEY SPILLANE

[1918-2006]

A LITERARY TOUGH GUY, HE CREATED THE CLASSIC DETECTIVE MIKE HAMMER

Mickey Spillane wielded words like a back-alley mugger swinging a blackjack. And if the critics didn't appreciate his work—which they didn't—well, that was their problem. "I pay no attention to those jerks," he told one interviewer. "I don't give a hoot about reading reviews," he said to another. "What I want to read are royalty checks." There were plenty. Brooklyn-born Spillane, who died July 17 at age 88, wrote his first book, *I, the Jury,* in 1947. It introduced his hard-drinking hero Mike Hammer. By 1980 seven of the Top 15 all-time bestselling fiction titles in America carried his byline; his novels have sold about 200 million copies worldwide.

GORDON PARKS [1912-2006]

LOOKING THROUGH THE VIEWFINDER, HE DISCERNED POVERTY AND OPPRESSION—AND USED HIS ART TO FIGHT THEM

In the late 1930s, Gordon Parks, then a waiter on the Northern Pacific Railroad, picked up a magazine a passenger had left behind. As he glanced through it, Parks, who died March 7, came across a photo spread of migrant workers—and was captivated. "I saw that the camera could be a weapon against poverty, against racism, against all sorts of social wrongs," he told an interviewer years later. "I knew at that point I had to have a camera." Inspired, the young high school dropout bought his first camera, a Voigtlander Brilliant, at a pawnshop, taught himself how to use it and embarked on a legendary career as a photojournalist, moviemaker and writer. Along the way, Parks became the first black photographer at LIFE magazine and *Vogue* and the first to write, score and direct a Hollywood movie (*The Learning Tree*). He also directed *Shaft*.

AL LEWIS

FANGS FOR THE MEMORIES: HE KNEW HOW TO PLAY SCARY FOR BIG LAUGHS

When he ran unsuccessfully for governor of New York State in 1998, he asked to be listed on the ballot as "Grandpa Al Lewis"—because almost everybody knew him as Grandpa Munster. Lewis, who died Feb. 3 at 82, achieved cult status in the 1960s as the 378-year-old paterfamilias of *The Munsters,* a role he seemed born to play. "His nose was really that big, his sideburns were that goofy," said son Ted, 41. "He and his character were really the same person."

MIKE [1925-2006] DOUGLAS

WITH AN EASYGOING TALK SHOW STYLE, HE BROUGHT THE STARS OUT IN DAYTIME

What did people watch before Oprah dominated TV's daylight hours? Most likely, in the '60s and '70s they caught *The Mike Douglas Show* and its eclectic array of guests. They saw John Lennon and Yoko Ono (who spent an entire week as cohosts), the Rolling Stones, Richard Nixon— as well as Mary Tyler Moore and Lucille Ball (pictured above) and, famously, a 2-year-old Tiger Woods. Douglas, who died Aug. 11 at age 81, began as a big-band singer (and had a pop hit in 1966 with "The Men in My Little Girl's Life"). By 1967 his daytime TV show would boast 6 million viewers. The secret of his success? Said Douglas: "I'm a square."

[1923-2006] DARREN McGAVIN

HE WAS TV'S MOST DOGGED INVESTIGATOR OF THINGS THAT GO BUMP IN THE NIGHT

When *The X-Files* creator Chris Carter needed an actor to play Arthur Dales, the obsessed FBI agent who started the files, he knew just whom to ask—McGavin, who, as an over-the-top Chicago reporter in 1974's *Kolchak: The Night Stalker*, inspired a whole school of paranoid there's-something-out-there TV storytelling. McGavin, who died on Feb. 25 at age 83, won an Emmy for playing Candice Bergen's father on *Murphy Brown* and gave a memorable performance in the 1983 Jean Sheperd holiday classic *A Christmas Story*. In the 1950s he had the distinction of starring in two hit TV shows at the same time—*Mike Hammer* and *Riverboat*. Playing the hard-boiled Hammer wasn't a challenge. "Hammer was a dummy," McGavin said. "I thought it was a comedy."

WILSON PICKETT

RAW PASSION AND HARD-EDGED ARTISTRY MADE HIM A SOUL LEGEND

He traveled all the way from a turbulent, poverty-ridden childhood in Prattville, Ala., to the Rock and Roll Hall of Fame and along the way recorded some of the most memorable soul songs of the '60s, including "Mustang Sally," "In the Midnight Hour" and "Land of 1,000 Dances." Pickett, who died Jan. 19 at age 64, moved to Detroit in the 1950s and, after starting out as a gospel singer, switched to a more earthy sound. "I wanted to sing gospel," he told an interviewer, "but I wanted to make me some money too." At the height of his career, he was mentioned in the same breath with such greats as Aretha Franklin, Otis Redding and Smokey Robinson. With the eclipse of soul music, Pickett's career took a downturn. Then, in the 1990s, sparked by worshipful mentions in the hit movie *The Commitments* and his induction into the Hall in 1991, he embarked on a comeback, introducing a new generation to his raspy-voiced pleasures.

RED BUTTONS [1919-2006]

HE STARTED OUT SMALL, STAYED SMALL, AND HAD A BIG CAREER AS AN ACTOR AND COMEDIAN

He was born Aaron Chwatt on Manhattan's Lower East Side. At 12, he sang onstage as Little Skippy. But as a high school student he got the name that made him famous—"Red" for his hair, "Buttons" for his bellhop uniform. Buttons, who died July 13 at 87, carved out a 70-year career as a song-and-dance man, comedian (he got his own CBS variety show in 1952) and actor—a Best Supporting Oscar for 1957's *Sayonara* and the role of his life in *The Poseidon Adventure*. But the diminutive Buttons knew the part that suited him best. "I'm a little guy," he once said, "and that's what I play."

Pickett (performing in his heyday) came back in 1999 with his Grammy-nominated album "It's Harder Now."

The many frazzled faces of Don Knotts (clockwise, from left): Barney Fife; Mr. Limpet; a would-be desperado in *The Fat Outlaw*; and host of *The Don Knotts Show*.

DON [1924-2006] KNOTTS

HEROIC! HANDSOME! STEADFAST! THAT'S WHAT HIS HAPLESS CHARACTERS THOUGHT THEY WERE

The Andy Griffith Show was supposed to be a vehicle for its star. But Knotts, playing bungling deputy sheriff Barney Fife, soon turned Griffith into a straight man. "Don meant everything," Griffith told *The Washington Post* after his sidekick's death on Feb. 24 at age 81. "Don made the show." Knotts specialized in playing deluded goofballs. The hyperventilating Barney Fife thought of himself as brave and resourceful. His *Three's Company* character, landlord Ralph Furley, usually resplendent in leisure suit and ascot, was under the illusion he was a lothario. Knotts also left a trove of movie roles, including *The Incredible Mr. Limpet, The Reluctant Astronaut* and *The Shakiest Gun in the West*. Said actor Tim Conway, his costar in *The Apple Dumpling Gang:* "He was the funniest guy I'd ever seen."

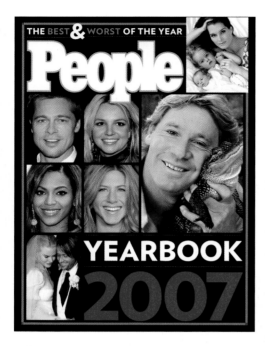

THE BEST & WORST OF THE YEAR
People
YEARBOOK 2007

CREDITS | 2006

TITLE PAGE
(from top) Splash News; Cookie Rosenberg/Retna

TABLE OF CONTENTS
(clockwise from top left) Troy Word; Ben Rose/Wireimage; BEImages; Barbara L. Johnston/AP

HEADLINERS
4-5 (clockwise from top left) AP (12); Courtesy of the Toler Family; Jeff Gentner/AP; **6-7** (clockwise from top left) Ed Reinke/AP; Chris Usher; Brendan Smialowski/EPA; Lingbing Hang/AP; **8-9** (from left) Animal Planet; Steve Holland/AP; **10-11** (clockwise from top left on 10) ABC News; Ida Mae Astute/ABC News; Michael Probst/AP (counterclockwise from top left on 11); CBS (3); Christian Science Monitor/AP; Eddie Seal/Bloomberg News/Landov; David Bohrer/White House/AP; **12-13** (from left) Carlo Allegri/Getty; Kevin Winter/Getty; **14-15** (clockwise from top left) Courtesy Taylor University (2); Joseph Kaczmarek/AP; Sabina Louise Pierce/University of Pennsylvania/EPA; Al Behrman/AP; Daniel Johnson/Marion Chronicle-Tribune/AP; **16-17** (clockwise from top of 16) ABC; Splash News; Wenn; Splash News; (clockwise from top of 17) James Estrin/The New York Times/Redux; Paul Sancya/AP; Pascal Rossignol/Reuters; Zuma (2); **18-19** (clockwise from left) Debra L. Rothenberg/Startraks; Peter Dejong/AP; Paul White/AP; **20-21** (clockwise from top left) E. M. Pio Roda/CNN/AP; Austrian Police/AP; Alfred Worm/Verlagsgruppe News; Austrian Police/AP; Chris Polk/FilmMagic; **22-23** (clockwise from left) Universal Studios; Jon Kopaloff/FilmMagic; Picture Media/INFGoff; Ramey; Flynet; LDP Images; Harpo; **24-25** (clockwise from left) Maisons Marques Domaines; Kristian Dowling/Getty; Kimberly French/Focus; **26-27** (clockwise from top left) Ellen Graham/Private Dreams of Public People; Miranda Shen/Globe; Patrick Simpson/Getty (2); Joseph Marzullo/Retna; **28-29** (from left) Elsa/Getty; Agence Zoom/Getty

CRIME
30-31 Mary Altaffer/AP (2); **32-33** (clockwise from top left on 32) Barbara L. Johnston/The Inquirer/AP;

Bradley C. Bower/Reuters; Pennsylvania State Police/AP; (from top on 33) Baldwin County Sheriff's Office/Reuters; Tennessee Bureau of Investigations/AP; **34-35** (clockwise from top left) Entwistle Family/AP; Bill Starling/Mobile Register/AP; Shelby County Sheriff's Office/AP (3); Joe Songer/Birmingham News/Polaris; Matt Campbell/EPA; **36-37** (from top on 36) Duke University/Zuma (3); Karl DeBlaker/AP; (from top on 37) Rungroj Yongrit/EPA/Corbis; Linda McConnell/Rocky Mountain News/Polaris; **38** (clockwise from top left) Boston Herald/Polaris; Mark Peterson/Redux; New York Department of Corrections/AP; **39** (clockwise from top left) Paul Connors/AP; Jack Kurtz/AP; Tomas Muscionico

WEDDINGS
40-41 Michael Brannigan; **42-43** Michael Brannigan (2); (clockwise from top on 43) Malibu Media (2); Eliot Press/Bauer-Griffin; **44-45** (clockwise from left) Cath Muscat/AAPimage/AP; Splash News (2); Don Arnold/Wireimage; Tracey Nearmy/AFP/Getty; **46-47** Andrew MacPherson (4); **48-49** Andrew MacPherson (5); **50-51** David Schumacher (4); **52-53** (clockwise from left) Lara Porzak and Heather Prichard; Robert Evans; Giles Harrison/Splash News; Eliot Press/Bauer-Griffin; **54-55** (from left) Splash News; (inset) Chopard; Ian Jones/Gamma; Chris Uncle/FilmMagic; **56** (from top) Joshua Dunbar Denniston; Vince Bucci/Getty; **57** Rebecca Bouck/ Wireimage; Mitch Haaseth/NBC (2)

BABIES
58-59 Getty; **60-61** Getty (2); **62-63** Troy Word (3); **64-65** (from left) Shavawn Rissman/AP; Marc Royce; **66-67** (from left) Marc Royce; **68-69** (clockwise from top left) Marc Royce; Tara Rochelle; Adrian Varnedoe/Pacific Coast News; **70-71** (from left) Ramey (3); Ken Katz; Vanity Fair

SPLITS
72-73 Alex Berliner/BEImages; Janet Gough/Celebrity Photo; **74-75** (clockwise from top left) Jordan Strauss/FilmMagic; Sonia Moskowitz/Globe; Tamara Beckwith/Splash News; Sunset Photo and News (2); **76-77** (clockwise from top left) Danny Moloshok/AP; /Thorpe/Bauer-Griffin; INF; Ginsburg-Spaly/X 17; Pacific Coast News; **78-79** Evening Standard; Daily Mirror (2); Rowan Griffiths (bottom left); Gregg DeGuire/Wireimage (right); **80-81** Rondeau/Presse Sports/Abaca; Billy Farrell/PMC; **82-83** (from left) Kevin Mazur/Wireimage; Axelle/Bauer-Griffin; Tsuni/Gamma; **84** Jamie McCarthy/Wireimage; David Edwards/DailyCeleb; **85** (from top); Tim Goodwin/Star Max; **86-87** (from left) Art Seitz-KPA/Zuma; Lester Cohen/Wireimage; Dan Steinberg/BEImages; **88-89** (clockwise from top left) Kevin Mazur/Wireimage; Tsuni/Gamma; REX USA

TV/MOVIES/MUSIC
90-91 Robert Trachtenberg; **92-93** (left to right) Michael Desmond/ABC; ABC; Michael Sharkey; Vivian Zink/ABC; Scott Garfield/ABC; **94-95** (clockwise from left) Peter Mountain/Disney; Kerry Hayes/Fox; Disney; **96-97** (clockwise from left) Sarah A. Friedman; Frank Micelotta/Getty; Mark Seliger/Sony; Gary Hershorn/Reuters; Gareth Davies/Getty; Terry Richardson/Jive

STYLE
98-99 Empics/Landov; **100-101** (from left) Jen Lowery/Startraks; Marcocchi

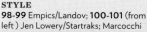

Giulio/Niviere/SIPA; Mario Anzuoni/Reuters; Hahn-Khayat-Nebinger/Abaca; Jill Johnson/JPI; Carmen Valdes/Photo Image Press; **102-103** (from left) Noel Hines/Landov; Tammie Arroyo/AFF; Frazer Harrison/Getty; Ramey; Sara De Boer/Retna; Lisa Rose/JPI; **104-105** (from left) Fitzroy Barrett/Landov; Tammie Arroyo/AFF; Tony Barson/Wireimage; Gilbert Flores/Celebrity Photo; Axelle/Bauer-Griffin; Roger Karnbad/Celebrity Photo; **106-107** (from left) Alba Montes/Loud and Clear Media; NPX/Star Max; Vince Bucci/Getty; Alba Montes/Loud and Clear Media; Michael Germana/SSI/Landov; Aaron Andrews/Photo Image Press; **108-109** (from left) Colin Knight/JPI; Jackson Lee/Splash News; Colin Knight/JPI; Peter Kramer/Getty; Dimitrios Kambouris/Wireimage; Jackson Lee/Splash News; **110-111** (from left) Frank Micelotta/Getty; Gilbert Flores/Celebrity Photo; Wenn; Matthew Imaging/FilmMagic; Tsuni/Gamma; Jason Merritt/FilmMagic; **112-113** Nancy Kaszerman/Zuma; Jamie McCarthy/Wireimage; Ronald Asadorian/Splash News; Nancy Kaszerman/Zuma; RE/Westcom/Star Max; Jason Merritt/FilmMagic; **114-115** (from left) Jackson Lee/Splash News; Lark/London Features; MB/X 17; Ramey; John Stanton/Wireimage; Sasha/X 17; Bryan Bedder/Getty

TRIBUTES
116-117 Ken Regan/Camera 5; Mary Ellen Mark; **118-119** (clockwise from top left) Olivier Douliery/Abaca USA; Jimi Celeste/PMC; Ken Regan/Camera 5; **120-121** Housez David/Gamma; **122-123** (from left) Globe; Corbis; Splash News; **124-125** Sam Jones/Corbis Outline; Neal Preston/Corbis; **126-127** Lynn McAfee/Globe; JP Laffont/Sygma/Corbis; **128-129** (from left) AP; Jeff Hyman/Shooting Star; AP; **130-131** (from left) Peter Serling; Getty; Robert Matheu/Retna; Neal Peters Collection/NBC; **132-133** (from left) Petar Kujundzic/Reuters; Peter Mazel/Sunshine/Retna; AP; **134-135** Douglas Kirkland/Corbis; Gordon Parks/FSA/Getty; **136-137** Universal/FF; MPTV; **138-139** Screen Scenes; Globe; **140-141** (clockwise from top left) Newscom; Hulton Archive/Getty; Screen Scenes; Photofest/Retna

"EVERY NIGHT IS LIKE
SUMMER VACATION.
IT'S THE MOST
AMAZING RUSH"
—KENNY CHESNEY ON THE JOYS OF LEADING
COUNTRY'S BIGGEST ROAD SHOW

"It's addictive,"
Chesney (at a Seattle
stadium show June 24)
says of the crowd's
energy. "To feel that
juice—it's amazing."

NOVEMBER 6. 2006

People

HEROES AMONG US
OUR 2006 AWARDS

NICOLE BY HIS SIDE

Keith's Struggle To Get Sober

Four months after their wedding, Urban seeks help to stop drinking. 'I deeply regret the hurt that this has caused Nicole'

GREY'S ANATOMY SCANDAL
What Really Happened

PAUL & HEATHER
Shocking Abuse Claims

$3.49US $4.79CAN

0 70989 10227 9   4 5>

www.people.com (AOL Keyword: People)

People

1962-2006
STEVE IRWIN'S
Tragic Death

A stingray barb through the heart kills the beloved Aussie adventurer, who leaves behind a wife and two children. How did this happen?

WOW! BODY AFTER BABY
How Stars Slim Down

MEREDITH VIEIRA
Ready for *Today*?

Jen: 'I'M NOT ENGAGED'

People

EXCLUSIVE INTERVIEW

SPECIAL REPORT
DID HE KILL JONBENET?

JOHN MARK KARR CONFESSES, BUT DOUBTS REMAIN
- Exclusive: his jailhouse interview
- What the evidence shows
- His bizarre obsessions

People

SPLIT!
KATE HUDSON & CHRIS ROBINSON
What Went Wrong

Exclusive! BRITNEY SPEAKS
MY LIFE AS A MOM

WITH BABY NO. 2 DUE ANY DAY, THE STAR REVELS IN SEAN PRESTON'S FIRST WORDS—AND FOOT RUBS FROM KEVIN

ROBIN WILLIAMS STRUGGLES TO GET SOBER

People

FALL 2006
STYLE WATCH

126 BUYS UNDER $100
Cute Shoes

SEXY HAIR
How to Get It

Kate's Style Secrets

SKINNY JEANS ARE BACK!
Yes, You Can Wear Them

Prettiest Tops

FALL FASHION
GREAT LOOKS GREAT PRICES
Plus! What's In, What's Out!

New Bags

People SPECIALS

People

LIFE AFTER SCOTT
Amber Frey Weds

IT'S BEEN A YEAR!

IS VINCE THE ONE?

The couple deny they're engaged. So what's up with that $500,000 diamond ring? The truth about Jen's very private romance

MALIBU!
Celeb Beach Party

JESSICA'S 26th B-Day Bash

SPECIAL DOUBLE ISSUE

People

BRITNEY
Defends Her Marriage

HOTTEST BACHELORS!
29 PAGES OF GREAT GUYS

AMERICAN IDOL'S
TAYLOR HICKS TELLS ALL ABOUT HIS
LOVE LIFE!

PAUL & HEATHER
Her Secret Past

PREACHER MURDER
His Wife In Court

People

MINERS TRIBUTE
Portraits of Bravery

EXCLUSIVE PICTURES!

ANGELINA REVEALS
'YES, I'M PREGNANT'

The star confirms she and Brad Pitt are expecting their first child

PINK'S Beach Wedding Album

HILARY SWANK'S
Surprise Split

OCTOBER 23. 2006

People

AMISH TRAGEDY
Portraits of Forgiveness

FARRAH BATTLES CANCER

Facing her sudden diagnosis, the *Angels* star begins treatment and leans on her ex, Ryan O'Neal. "She's so strong," he says. "I love her all over again"

KATIE HOLMES
She Has Her Wedding Dress!

ANGELINA JOLIE
On Location in India

MARCH 6. 2006

People

JESSICA & NICK
DIVORCE BATTLE!

So much for parting amicably: Both sides trade charges as a struggle looms over the ex-couple's money and property

TOM & KATIE
The Wedding Is Still On

HILARY & CHAD
Trying to Work It Out

LISA MARIE PRESLEY
Marries in Japan